£1.99

Sally Garratt became a~~~~ ~~~~
after gaining considerabl~~~~
ceutical industry and wit~~~~
has travelled regularly t~~~~
a director of Organisatio~~~~
sultancy based in Hong ~~~~
husband, Bob Garratt, on assignments relating to Board and
director development and organizational change in Hong
Kong, Brunei, Singapore, Mauritius, Australia, New Zealand, Sweden and the UK. They helped to set up the
ASEAN-EC Management Centre based in Brunei. They
have visited China often since 1976 on private trips or leading AMED Study Tours, and were involved in the establishment of the EEC/China Business School in Beijing in 1984.

Sally has designed and run development programmes for
senior professional and executive women, training courses
in personal effectiveness/time management and inter-
viewing skills, and worked with sixth formers on 'Insight
into Industry' and 'Challenge of Management' courses. She
has also written sales training programmes and carried out
research for television programmes and the construction
industry.

Sally has a degree in Malay and Anthropology from
London University. She is the author of *Going it Alone: How
to Thrive and Survive as an Independent Consultant* and *Manage
Your Time*, and co-author with her husband of *China Business
Briefing*. She also carried out the research for the *Economist's
Guide to Management Consultants*.

...became an independent consultant in 1978... ...work experience in the pharma-... ...in design practices. Since 1979 she... ...East and South East Asia and is... ...Organisation Development Ltd, an HR con-... ...in Hong Kong. She has worked with her...

WOMEN MANAGING
FOR THE
MILLENNIUM

Sally Garratt

HarperCollinsBusiness
An Imprint of HarperCollins*Publishers*

HarperCollinsBusiness
An imprint of HarperCollins*Publishers*
77–85 Fulham Palace Road,
Hammersmith, London W6 8JB

A Paperback Original 1998
1 3 5 7 9 8 6 4 2

A catalogue record for this book
is available from the British Library

ISBN 0 00 638677 6

Set in Linotype Meridien by
Rowland Phototypesetting Ltd,
Bury St Edmunds, Suffolk

Printed and bound in Great Britain by
Caledonian International Book Manufacturing Ltd, Glasgow

To all those women managers who;
in the past, have paved the way for the rest of us;
in the present, are reaping the benefits of that pioneering
work and taking it forward;
and, in the future, will recognize the contribution of
previous generations and be able to realize for
themselves our dreams and hopes for fulfilling,
challenging and balanced lives.

And to:

All the men who are working for a world where diversity
is valued and where each individual's skills and talents
are used and appreciated.

CONTENTS

Acknowledgements   ix

Introduction   1

PART ONE: How Did We Get Here?   13

**WOMEN AT WORK: THE WAY IN, THE WAY
    UP AND THE WAY FORWARD**   15

MANAGEMENT BARRIERS
Attitudes of organizations and managers   18
Lack of career guidance and career goals   25
Family pressures and expectations   35
Personal limitations   40

HELP IS AT HAND
Colleagues   47
Family   50
Role models, coaches and mentors   51
Friends and networks   54
Books and articles   56
Courses and outside activities   58

EMBRACING CHANGE
The nature of learning   64
Finding the right training   65
Women-only programmes   71

CRITERIA FOR SUCCESS
How do we measure success?   79

KEEPING THE BALANCE

PART TWO: Managing for the Millennium   93

**THE 21st-CENTURY MANAGER: THE
   SHAPE OF THINGS TO COME**   95

LOOKING FORWARD
How could training and development for women
   managers be improved?   104
Do women need to compromise to succeed in
   a male-dominated corporate world?   114
A seat on the board?   118
And, finally . . .   124

Appendix I: The Case Studies   127
Appendix II: The Scope of the Questionnaire   131
Appendix III: Questionnaire   135

Further Reading   157

Useful addresses   161

Index   169

ACKNOWLEDGEMENTS

It's impossible for me to acknowledge by name many of those who have helped me with this book. They are the people I've spoken with, listened to, lived with, fought against, been influenced by, laughed and cried with over the past fifty years. They've all affected the way I dealt with being a girl from a potentially disruptive background, being brought up by a remarkable mother who was determined that my brother and I should fulfil our capabilities and ambitions. They've all inspired me to seek out and tackle new challenges and then helped me to deal with, and learn from, the consequences, whether happy or disappointing.

Specific thanks go to the women who completed the questionnaire: Vivienne Avery, Sophie Brewer, Jan Burns, Caroline Cayzer, Janice Cook, Jill Dodwell-Groves, Margaret Elward, Judith Evans, Paula Fance, Sheila Forbes, Sally Fraser, Gay Haskins, Caroline Highwood, Sally Irvine, Wendy Kear, Pauline Kingi, Caroline Leigh, Jaki Meekings, Janice Morton, Virginia Novarra, Sharon Lee Polledri, Hilary Rowland, Marjorie Scardino, Christine Smart and Gill Sutherland. I am indebted to those who, in addition, provided material for the case studies: Theresa Barnett, Sarah Beech, Julia Budd, Carol Gladwin, Beverley Fowle, Judy Oliver, Zoë Reed, Sarah Sharratt and Alison Thorne. Most of the quotes used in the book are theirs – which means they are really my co-authors. My thanks also go to

Susan Hay who has been involved in childcare provision over the last decade and who gave me her views on how it has evolved over that period. The good-natured co-operation of all these women has made this exercise a hugely enjoyable and informative experience. I am pleased and proud to have been able to include them in this book – I hope they approve of the result.

I am grateful to Elisabeth Henderson and her colleagues at the Recess College for taking the time in the middle of a busy programme to update the details of the college.

Lady Howe, chairman of Opportunity 2000, and Viki Holton at Ashridge Management were generous with their time and assistance during my research – I greatly appreciated their enthusiasm, especially as they must face endless enquiries on a daily basis.

Additional thanks to all the women who worked with me on a workshop at the AMED Annual Conference in April 1997; they provided me with many of the examples and thoughts I needed to tie up loose ends in the text.

Thanks go to Lucinda McNeile and Emma Harrison-Topham of HarperCollins for having the faith to commission the book and for their unfailing patience when the computer crashed and my time management skills failed!

My husband, Bob, is always there to set an example of how rewarding it is to be generous with time and support. He, together with family, friends and colleagues, make almost anything possible!

Final and most heartfelt thanks go to my mother, Jean, who always makes me believe that I can achieve whatever I set out to do.

WOMEN MANAGING FOR THE MILLENNIUM

INTRODUCTION

The role of women in the world of work, and the consequent impact it will have on corporate cultures, is at a crucial transitional point as we approach the Millennium. How organizations respond will determine to a large extent the future of business and the economic success of the nation.

The world of work is undergoing a significant transformation and is learning, through necessity, to manage that change. Organizations of all sizes are rethinking not only how they are structured but, above all, how they are run and what types of directing and managing styles are appropriate.

Growing recognition and acceptance that women bring different and unique talents to the workplace has resulted in women making remarkable headway in organizations during the latter years of this century. That awareness must now be taken a step further – by fully integrating men and women within corporate cultures – so that organizations may reap the benefit of the combination of both sexes' abilities and qualities.

First, the statistics: all indicators point to significant changes in the future composition of the working population of the United Kingdom. *Social Trends 27* – the 1997 edition of the annual survey of life in the UK published by the Office for National Statistics – reports that, by 2006, the number of full-time jobs is not expected to show any significant increase or decrease, but that the existing trend for more part-time and self-employed workers is likely to be reinforced.

It is anticipated that, by 2006, women will account for 46% of the entire workforce; and of the additional 1.4 million people expected in the workforce, 1 million will be women. The number of part-time workers is set to rise by 10% and those in self-employment by 25%. Traditionally, women are more likely to be in part-time work, but that trend, too, is changing. Between 1986 and 1996, the numbers of women in part-time work rose by 17% to 5.3 million, but the number of men doubled to 1.2 million. *Social Trends 27* also reports that, in 1995, the UK had a higher proportion of people working from home than any other EU country, with 30% of males and 25% of females working at home for at least part of the year.

If these statistics are borne out, then the number of women within all spheres of the workplace will increase dramatically and the nature of organizations will undoubtedly change. As modern companies recognize the need to be people-oriented and family-friendly in order to move forward and succeed, they will need to build on the 'feminine' characteristics which complement the 'masculine' traits that have traditionally typified corporate cultures. The workplace would then not drive women away, but become much more attractive to them.

As society re-evaluates the way it conducts itself, and as businesses search for healthier ways of organizing themselves, the old ways are being called into question. Characteristics of traditional, male-dominated organizations – where women have been judged by masculine yardsticks – are no longer accepted as the norm. The competitive, controlling, hierarchical, dictatorial, critical approaches epitomized by the Army, the Church and the State, and practised by many business organizations, are being strongly challenged by supporters of the more intuitive feminine qualities of co-operation, facilitation, coaching and an ability to listen to and encourage other people.

Already, a great number of highly successful women have paved the way to a point where their influence is beginning to be felt and appreciated. Marjorie Scardino, Chairman of the Pearson Group, has become the first female chairman of a FT-SE 100 company. By example, such women have highlighted alternative approaches to the traditional managerial styles of the past, and are teaching organizations to react positively in their attitudes to employing women. In turn, organizations are accepting that women's capabilities provide a useful, complementary and necessary foil to the skills and qualities of their male employees. This is why there is such a strong and determined move towards establishing equality of opportunity in the workplace.

In the aftermath of the publication of GCSE and A level results in 1994, there were several articles remarking on the fact that girls' schools had 'forged ahead' in the league tables. In an article featured in *The Times* of 3 September 1994, a professor of education was quoted as saying 'Ten years of equal opportunities has focused on raising the standards achieved by girls, and has proved brilliantly successful.'

This trend has continued to the point where girls in all types of school have been outperforming the boys at GCSE and are now beginning to do so at A level, too. In the spring of 1996, the Chief Inspector of Schools described the under-achieving of boys as one of the most disturbing problems facing the education system. Schools are now having to turn their attention to raising the standards of boys' work, but understand that they will have to tackle the problem in a fresh way – taking into account the specific needs and culture of boys' groups, whilst maintaining girls' progress – thereby allowing the two groups to work together naturally and to the benefit of both.

We are reminded that this is undoubtedly a period of dramatic change, time and time again, through the reactions of the media, the presence of ever-successful management gurus and the constant demand for training courses. The result of this turbulence is that the majority of us have experienced the consequences, either stimulating or depressing, of those changes and, if we have not been affected directly, we know someone who has.

The shape and structures of organizations are altering rapidly as we move towards the twenty-first century. This may manifest itself in the transformation from public to corporatized or privatized companies, from strict hierarchies to flatter structures, or from centralized to de-centralized businesses.

As this trend continues, organizations increasingly have to look at new ways of working; of how to react continuously to the turbulence around them, internally and externally, and, above all, how to *learn* from all these experiences.

Directors, senior managers and executives are facing difficult questions and dilemmas about the best way to meet these challenges. This is especially true as employees are beginning to reel from the effects of too much change and are instead looking forward to a period of consolidation where new ways of working and operating are given a chance to succeed.

Organizations suffer when their workforce begins to feel jaded and worn down by continuous upheaval. It becomes difficult to judge the relative success or failure of different initiatives if they have not been subjected to rigorous benchmarking before more changes occur, if they are not given time to work, or if insufficient thought to their introduction means they are not properly implemented.

Newspapers, journals, TV and radio, and the professional associations which deal primarily with the management and direction of organizations are looking carefully at how the art of managing will evolve over the next few years. *Management Development to the Millennium* (1996), published by the Institute of Management, says that 'he (The Boss) is just as likely to be a she, because female ways of managing will be more appropriate in the millennium'.

One of the key features of change already in place is the implosion of middle management, which indicates that the emphasis of the managerial role is being altered. Many traditional roles, such as personnel, administration and accounting, have been devolved to line managers who consequently find that their jobs now include extra tasks for which they may be ill-equipped. The combination of an increased sphere of responsibility and often only a superficial knowledge of their new tasks can result in feelings of professional anxiety and insecurity unless they adapt their management style from *coercing* and *telling* to *co-operating* and *encouraging*. This is where women will come into their own.

Yet, at a time when women are increasingly seen to be treated on an equal footing with their male counterparts, there are rumblings of discontent among the ranks of women managers about the world of work within which they are expected to operate. Many successful women managers are beginning to realize that achieving high corporate status is not as rewarding as they anticipated and they are baulking at the idea of giving up their entire lives to an organization.

In 1997, it was reported in the press on both sides of the Atlantic that the President and Chief Executive of PepsiCo, Brenda Barnes, had decided to stand down from her highly prestigious job in order to spend time watching her sons play football. She is only one of a series of established and successful career women who have decided that they cannot, or do not want to, 'have it all' – the concept championed by Nicola Horlick, the City financier who claims that women can combine a high-flying career with a strong marriage and successful motherhood.

The question, as far as many women are concerned, is not '*can* we have it all?' but 'do we *want* to have it all?'

What has caused this transitional stage? Why should women be discontented just as they are beginning to achieve what they have been aiming for over so many years? And, if this trend continues, where will it leave women's position within the workplace?

But, while it is true that many women managers are fighting a daily battle for recognition and equality of opportunity at work, it is also clear that others are increasingly able to grow and develop. Progress is being made as attitudes, together with company structures, change in women's favour. We have, at least, moved away from the situation which existed up until the late 1950s and early 1960s when guides for graduates clearly indicated which companies did not employ females. Men are becoming more family conscious. Women have mentioned the increasing number of male bosses who, with families of their own, are more sympathetic to their female colleagues' attempts to achieve a tenable balance between work, home and leisure. I hope this book gives heart and shows what is possible. Perhaps for those who are unable to change the status quo of where they work now, merely knowing that more enlightened people and organizations do exist will be encouragement enough for those who are unhappy with their current situation to look for jobs elsewhere. This, and the need to re-educate and re-train men, is now seen as urgent if equality of opportunities is to become a reality.

As the attitudes of society and employers towards child-care provision and parenting also develop and improve, more choices will be open to employees to begin to achieve the desired balance of home, leisure and work that is one of the major causes of stress among women today. Susan Hay, a leading provider of workplace nurseries, has seen many changes over the past ten years and suggests that women have become more successful at making their jobs work for them. 'I suppose the fact is that people who are in work do work very hard. They have become more valuable and companies want to keep them. You get the feeling that there is not nearly as much deadwood as there was, so the people who are in work are in a strong position to make sense of their working lives and, provided they can demonstrate that the employer is gaining rather than losing from an arrangement, they do at least receive a warm hearing. The facts are that women are becoming more tenacious and there is a change in approach by HR people. I think these two trends have come together quite well.'

Part and parcel of an important drive towards building an effective workforce – with the consequent positive effect on the bottom line – is an initiative launched in October 1991 to advance the causes of women at work, Opportunity 2000. This campaign, chaired by Lady Howe, has one clear objective: to increase the quality and quantity of women's employment opportunities in both private and public sector organizations. There are currently 293 members representing over 25% of the UK workforce. As an example of what the campaign has achieved, listed below are some figures relating to women at work, taken from the 1994/95 review of members' progress:

- the percentage of women directors in member organizations has doubled in one year from 8% to 16%
- women now account for 32% of all managers – up from 25% last year
- the percentage of women in senior management is up from 12% to 17%, and middle managers from 24% to 28%
- 45% of all graduate entrants are women

Opportunity 2000 also makes positive steps towards recognizing and publicizing the achievement of organizations in increasing the participation of women in the workforce by giving awards to businesses which show demonstrable progress in this field. In 1997, for example, they awarded Yorkshire Bank an award for 'dismantling the glass ceiling'. When a new chief executive arrived at the bank, he was shocked by the bank's poor record on promoting women. He and the equal opportunities manager introduced a scheme whereby female employees were encouraged to seek promotion and this has increased the number of women moving into the first level of management by 29% in a year. The chief executive points out that this scheme is rooted in straightforward business sense and that, if 70% of the people in the bank were women, then the bank would not be able to achieve its objectives if it drew its management only from the other 30% of the workforce.

A report, *A Question of Balance? A survey of managers' changing professional and personal values*, discusses the gap between managers and their organizations in terms of the cultural values which impact on performance. Modern managers are seen to hold positive attitudes which do not sit comfortably alongside the less enlightened cultures still found in many businesses.

Even though the business environment is changing to enable 'female ways of managing' to develop, I suspect that we lost a whole generation of women managers during the 1980s – probably because many of the women who reached the top during that self-centred, brittle decade did not help and support other women and may have, on occasions, actively impeded their progress. This has also resulted in many of the surviving fifty-plus year-olds saying that they have little in common with the younger women and either feel more in tune with their male peers, or feel completely isolated. Now, however, there is a strong feeling that this attitude is disappearing and that successful women are increasingly aware of the need to broadcast their achievements and act as role models, coaches and mentors for the up and coming generation.

We should also bear in mind that, as long as women tend not to measure success solely in terms of status, money and celebrity, there will not be equal numbers of men and women at senior management level. We need to think in terms of equal satisfaction in what women managers are achieving. An example of women's broader approach is, 'Although I was in a very senior, prestigious position, I have recently taken a (slightly) downwards step to another post in order to improve the quality of my private life and to maximize the time available for it. That was probably the hardest career decision I have ever taken'. I suspect that women would score higher on this criterion than the men, although it is true that the men are beginning to realize the issues and change their behaviours.

I feel, however, that the real differences will become clear as the current generation of teenagers moves into the world of work. I recently spent some time with the sixth formers at a co-ed public school and was impressed with the attitudes of the boys and girls towards the concept of working together. One of the issues we discussed at length was the occasional pitfalls of men and women working together in business and I was heartened by the positive and sensitive attitudes of both boys and girls to the subject. In fact they almost dismissed it, as it seemed obvious to them that working together on an equal footing was the natural and sensible way of doing things.

I sincerely hope that, as they encounter the current prejudices in organizational cultures, they will have the courage to hold on to the partnership idea and carry it through their lives at work, at home and at play. I trust that the boys won't be persuaded to adopt the superior, 'macho' views of their male colleagues and managers and that the girls will not lose their self-confidence and begin to believe that they are the passive, second-class sex.

If our hopes for the future lie with these young people, then we have to do all we can to pass on what we have learned so that they, too, may learn and take that learning forward to the benefit of everyone.

I have been working with young people and feel strongly about the need to equip them to deal with the changing world of work. I now want to assess the changes that have affected women in management so that they may:

- learn from the past and present and so approach the future confidently, with full knowledge of the challenges they will have to face
- clarify how they may contribute fully to managing their organizations, businesses and communities as they strive to survive and flourish in the next century.

There is a feeling of optimism about the future for women in business. This revolves around an increasing compatibility between the sexes in the workplace, rather than the unrealistic expectation that male and female managers will ever be equal in numbers. The domestic factor of female employees with families is the main reason for this, although 'family-friendly' employment policies are gaining some ground. It is also significant that more and more women are either setting up their own small businesses, or becoming self-employed, as an alternative to having to fit into a corporate culture which is, for many, an alien way of working.

Demographic pressures and trends, education, male views of sharing family responsibilities, among other issues, are all building towards a peak that suggests we are on the brink of a fundamental change in the role women will play in the world of management. Women must prepare themselves to make full use of these changes and the consequent opportunities to take their appropriate places as directors and managers. They will introduce female perspectives and behaviours to complement those currently held in traditional, male-dominated organizations and bring a much-needed balance to the corporate world, thus enabling it to be more successful in its competitive environment.

Women are now in a position to excel as they grow in confidence and begin to understand the benefits of diversity in the workplace. As one manager says, 'All successful women need to share their experiences – tips on success, motivation and confidence, as well as revealing failures – so all women will see it is not an easy ladder to climb'. They will, however, see that it is possible to climb that ladder.

Networking and the need for coaches and mentors have also been mentioned time and time again as an important way of building up a store of experiences which may be used to increase confidence in two ways: first, that to employ behaviours with which you feel comfortable is the best approach and, second, that you have learned and absorbed all the skills and knowledge required to do the job.

What I hope will prove interesting and helpful are the comments and opinions of women who have found themselves in a variety of situations and how they have dealt with them. They are typical of the many thousands of women managers throughout the country who have a strong feeling of their worth and who are beginning to make their presence felt.

Through the examples of case studies and interviews, through long discussions with friends and work colleagues, through articles in various publications and from my own experiences as an employee, manager, teacher, developer, trainer, and consultant to organizations, my aim in this book is threefold:

1 to look at what has happened to women managers in the past so that we may learn from their experiences

2 to set the benchmarks of where women managers are now and where they would like/expect to be as we approach the next century (because only if we do that will we know later if any change has actually taken place)

3 to suggest ways in which women may prepare themselves for the different environments of the next century

It is crucial that women

- become aware of the major challenges facing management
- understand what qualities and skills managers will need to deal with those challenges
- discuss what women, in particular, will bring to the different organizational structures and cultures
- work with men to achieve the balance and strength that diversity brings

Having learned from the past and present, women can approach the future confidently knowing what challenges they will have to face, and how they can contribute fully to managing their organizations, businesses and communities in the next century.

PART ONE
How did we get here?

WOMEN AT WORK:
THE WAY IN, THE WAY UP
AND THE WAY FORWARD

The career paths of a great many of today's women managers often seem to have their beginnings rooted in a haphazard past. In the early 1960s, when I sat my A levels and wondered what I was going to do next, the career counsellors at my grammar school concluded that I was not university material and suggested I went to secretarial college. The choice was that or teacher training college or becoming a nurse. I believed the counsellors when they said I wasn't clever enough to go to university, and having no idea of what the future might hold and feeling relieved to have got that far anyway, I went along with the idea of doing a one-year secretarial course in London.

For me the secretarial route proved to be an excellent way of moving into junior management and large numbers of my contemporaries (many of whom are now public figures) followed the same path. Today many parents actively dissuade their daughters from taking a secretarial course, primarily because they still perceive the role of secretary as the demeaning stereotype, or because they believe it has no prospects for a 'proper' job. Perhaps with more people learning keyboard skills within a job, good secretarial training – and the accompanying self-organization skills – are not seen to be as important in the workplace as they once were.

Another traditional way into management was via personnel and training and, until recently, many senior women in the private sector represented the human resources field. Some took the secretarial administration route, while others began as graduate trainees, choosing personnel as their preferred specialism. While personnel was somehow understood to be less 'difficult' than other areas of a company, and the 'sharing and caring' skills of personnel were always seen to be the preserve of women, it is now quite usual to find women managers in all other aspects of business, such as engineering, finance, law and marketing.

In the public sector, the health service has a markedly different male/female ratio among its managers from that of the private sector. This does not automatically mean that women have an easier time moving up the career structure, but it does indicate that they are probably more experienced at working with male colleagues who are, in turn, more used to working with women. 'One of the reasons I have enjoyed working in the NHS is because I have always felt that equal recognition is given to good managers, regardless of their sex. There are excellent managers of both sexes in the NHS – it is very much up to the individuals to create their own opportunities.'

Many of the women managers I have met from the NHS, or local authorities, have spent the greater part of their working lives within the same organization, but have regularly changed jobs within it. They have gained invaluable experience from this, especially in learning how to keep an eye open for appropriate openings and in seizing any available opportunity for advancement and personal development.

As I mentioned in the introduction, there are increasing numbers of women who will no longer tolerate a strictly male management environment. But, having challenged the 'jobs for the boys' culture and moved up the corporate ladder, then many women, halfway through their careers, opt out.

Why do so many women having made it to middle management fail to take their careers and their management skills any further up the corporate ladder? The explanations for this include: lack of confidence and not pushing themselves forward; career breaks; the glass ceiling; not going on courses; being late developers (recognizing their abilities at a later stage than their male contemporaries); and being unwilling to play internal politics or 'men's games'.

The main points characterizing women's current positions as managers, particularly those over 35, seem to be:

- career counselling, coaching and mentoring were not nearly as sophisticated in the early 1960s–70s as they are now
- the range of available jobs has broadened out immeasurably due to change in society's attitudes generally, self-confidence and aspirations of individuals
- for many managers in their late thirties/forties/fifties, the career path to management is haphazard/snakes and ladders, with the necessary skills being picked up along the way
- nowadays, careers are and have to be better planned, with the emphasis on an open mind. This means focusing on acquiring skills through experience and training rather than aiming for a particular job level in one particular industry

MANAGEMENT BARRIERS

Women managers identify four main reasons for late entry into managerial roles, or for slow progress in achieving their career goals:

- Attitudes of organizations and managers (male and female)

- Lack of career guidance/career goals
- Family pressures and expectations
- Personal limitations

Attitudes of organizations and managers

Not surprisingly, women have found it particularly hard to progress within traditionally male-dominated cultures and organizational structures. They talk of 'men and their perceptions of who and what is needed and the way to do things'. One human resources specialist spoke of 'a company culture which is particularly hierarchical, conservative and control-oriented. This has made life difficult for me, given that my career has been about valuing human resources as a strategic and developmental activity.'

Women may come up against male prejudices at work in all manner of guises. Organizations which operate graduate traineeships and management schemes for 'high fliers' often tend to favour male Oxbridge graduates. One woman who was employed by such a company realized that being female and coming from an ex-polytechnic was so abhorrent to one of the male managers that he consequently successfully obstructed her progress within the company.

During my research, I heard numerous examples whereby male managers had deliberately excluded women colleagues from management team meetings, or had discussed important issues away from formal meetings so that women were not involved. Such feelings of discomfort and threat or fear of the unknown are experienced by many men when they face working closely with women – possibly for the first time – and they may employ tactics such as using their stronger, louder voices to drown out female colleagues in an attempt to halt their contributions. It is not unusual for the credit of a woman's work to be taken by her male boss or colleague, but it is becoming less acceptable to excuse such behaviour on the grounds of male feelings of jealousy or vulnerability, or because men are assumed to be following their instincts to dominate, protect and provide.

One woman's experience was:

> 'There were two male managers who were in competition with each other over my work and resources and over who wanted to use my achievements to advance themselves. They always managed to keep themselves promoted ahead of me so my work could keep pushing them forward.'

A chilling example of some male managers' attitudes is given by a woman working in the NHS:

> 'I was aware there were helpful females in my own organization, but I was actively prevented by male managers from gaining legitimate access to them.'

One common experience shared by women managers is the failure to secure a deserved promotion or a higher level job, knowing that, in spite of the official reasons given, it came down to the fact that they were not male. Specific examples of this emerged from an ambitious local government officer who felt strongly that she would have reached the position of Chief Executive by now if she were a man, and another manager who was told: 'On the face of it you have every-thing the job needs, but, you see, it wouldn't do to have a woman. We're not ready for that yet'. That was in 1986.

In spite of legislation, these practices still exist, albeit covertly, because employees in less enlightened and open organizations are aware that they could be subjected to charges of sexual discrimination, harassment and so on.

One of this book's case study interviewees, Carol, had always said that she had rarely come across discrimination, probably because she never expected it, but she does have one personal example which she relates: 'When the children were younger, I employed a nanny and one day, when she was ill, I grabbed some work and told my boss I had to collect the children. I did the work at home, but when I went back into the office the next day he said, "This is a problem. How do I know that this isn't going to happen again?" I said, "How dare you. You gave one of the men in the department a week off work because his wife had hurt her back. You were all sympathy for him. The person who was looking after the children was ill – it's the same situation". He then saw my point and no more was said.'

Another interviewee, Judy, qualified as a barrister in the late 1970s but found that, in addition to there being too many barristers on the market, there were problems in being a woman in the law. She did not fit in with the stereotype set by the men – nor did she want to. Most of all she disliked the lack of sensitivity towards clients – what she called the 'legal equivalent of a bedside manner'. When she tried to change the attitudes of those she worked with, she was totally ignored and moved from the legal department of her organization into a management training role. In spite of her many successes, 'I was starting to experience problems with a boss who was finding my innovative approach both disconcerting and a threat. He realized that women's issues was a topical subject that he should address but, although I was the only woman in my team with relevant experience of these, I was never asked to contribute'.

At the top of organizations, the unwillingness to appoint women to the board is commonplace. The experience of one director who was not promoted to her board despite seven years on the Group Executive Committee is not unusual. Private sector organizations, in particular, are seen as traditionally conservative, with chairmen appointing fellow board members in their own image – same background, same sex, same education, same professional training, same age. This lack of diversity, however, is now becoming subject to scrutiny and criticism, especially following publications such as the Cadbury Committee report which recommends the widespread use of non-executive, or independent, directors on boards. Growing numbers of experienced, professional women are proving valuable additions to boards across a wide range of business activities.

Yet it is not just the male managers who prove obstructive. Those women who, in the past, felt they could progress within their organizations only by becoming 'honorary men' affected other women in two ways. First, as many of them adopted the 'I reached this position through my own efforts. Why should I help you?' attitude, they positively impeded their junior colleagues' progress. Second, this approach deterred many other women from moving forward as it was not seen as an acceptable way of behaving. The role model presented by these power-dressing, aggressive female managers was not perceived as a positive one and other women did not, therefore, feel inclined to apply for more senior jobs.

I was interested to hear one fifty-year-old executive, who is the only woman at her level in the organization, say that she feels she has little in common with other, much younger, female managers and that there are none anywhere near her age or experience. Because of her position she naturally has more contact with her male peers on a day-to-day basis, but she feels she is missing out by not working with other women. One disadvantage of the recent fashion for 'down-sizing' and 'right-sizing' is that there are signs of a small, but significant, counter-trend where some women have been forced out of top-level posts and those who remain may well find themselves in a similar situation of becoming isolated and lonely. Other women say that in such cases it is the duty of the older female manager to act as a mentor or coach to others as a way of helping them through the organization, as well as keeping in touch with the issues that affect the younger women – such as, how to communicate their opinions and needs in a positive, assertive manner, while maintaining their womenliness; combining home and work; influencing the corporate culture so that men and women value what they each bring to the workplace.

Very few companies provide adequate if any childcare arrangements for their employees. This has a considerable effect on working mothers, who wish to pursue their career but who are not prepared to settle for unsatisfactory childcare facilities in order to continue working. Susan Hay, who founded her own workplace nursery consultancy because she could not find suitable childcare for her own children, has ten years' experience in this field and knows that the position of working women has been hindered because of the lack of investment in childcare by organizations. 'Access to childcare, as well as the cost and varying quality of it, has been a major influence on the development and expansion of part-time work for women. This often means that women are working below their abilities because the better jobs are full-time jobs. There is also a tendency for higher-level jobs to be in the key cities and this is not always compatible with acceptable childcare provision.'

The growing importance of childcare issues was underlined in November 1997, when the Chancellor of the Exchequer, Gordon Brown, announced the establishment over the next five years of 300,000 'After School Clubs', which will offer places to up to one million children.

Case study – Alison

Alison, 41, is married with no children. She trained as a nurse and worked as a medical secretary, before moving into the field of management education and training. She was the founding director of a medical charity; set up a management consultancy; founded her own charity, Action on Depression; and is Director of the British Vascular Foundation. She was a former Chair-

man of City Women's Network, and has served on the Women's
Advisory Panel of Opportunity 2000 and on the board of Fair
Play for Women. She is a trained counsellor; Fellow of the RSA;
a member of the National Association of Chief Executives of
National Voluntary Organizations; and also sits on the board
of The International Alliance (a global organization of senior
women's networks).

'My girls' public school had few expectations for its pupils
and after leaving I became a nurse. I wanted to live in
London and to be self-supporting after all the financial sacri-
fices my parents had made to pay my school fees, but I
couldn't stand the rigid hierarchy at the hospital where I
worked and felt totally unstretched intellectually. I realized
that I should have read medicine, not nursing, but financially it was not possible to give up work to take the necessary
A levels, nor did I have the confidence to make the switch.
After qualifying, I became a staff nurse at Guy's, but at the
back of my mind was always the niggling thought – "Is the
rest of my life going to be like this?"

'I decided to give myself a year away from hospitals to
see what was happening in the outside world and thought
again about studying medicine. I have always regretted not
doing it. With the misguided idea that becoming a secretary
would be a clear route into management, I enrolled for a
six-week typing course and invented my own shorthand. I
boldly put myself forward as a medical secretary and went
to work in a hospital where I was tucked away in a back
office with only the occasional consultant for company. This
was not at all exciting – there wasn't even the patient contact that I had so enjoyed as a nurse. So, making yet another
mistake, I joined a firm of accountants because I thought
it would be fun in the City. It was very jolly there, but my
boss fell in love with me and, as I wasn't interested and
three years of accountants was ample, I left to help set up
a private medical screening facility. It was the first of its

kind and I soon realized that I actually possessed some entrepreneurial talents and obviously enjoyed starting new projects. However, once it was up and running successfully, I thought, "Where do we go from here? All this experience, no clear career path, no way to use the experience, so what should I do next?"

'I was twenty-seven, had spent ten years in London and was bored, footloose and fancy free. I had the urge to go abroad again (as the daughter of a naval officer, I travelled a great deal), so I stuck a pin in a map and hit Hong Kong. I had no job planned, nowhere to live and not much money, but six weeks later I was on a plane. Hong Kong is a sink-or-swim place and there is nothing so motivating as having no money. The most useful thing that happened was being introduced to a residential club for business-women, the Helena May, where a group of us shared experiences, jobs, contacts and so on. I nursed for a short while, but felt even more exploited than I had done in the UK, so was soon looking for something else. Through the Helena May network, I went to a cocktail party and met a businessman who ran training courses and who had been badly let down by one of his tutors – who should have been running a programme in China, but had been taken ill. After talking for a while, he asked if I would like to take the tutor's place – "Can you be on the 8.30 flight tomorrow morning?" Having agreed, I found myself in what felt like the middle of nowhere with sixty hand-picked Chinese executives who were there to learn about Western management methods. It was exciting, frustrating and I loved it. I developed a great love of China, in spite of developing malnutrition, surviving banquets of three-snake casserole and sea cucumber, and went on to learn Mandarin at the Chinese University of Hong Kong. Later, I was headhunted to set up the Asian arm of an American computer company and my boss delegated everything so I ran the whole show.

'Between contracts working in China and return trips to

Hong Kong for much needed R&R, I went to a tea party and met my husband. We were married in England while still living in Hong Kong – so don't ever complain about organizing a big wedding, unless you've arranged it from a distance of 8000 miles! I was thirty-three and keen to stay in Hong Kong, but my husband wanted to come home. I had been away for five or six years and felt very out of touch – the sort of things I had been doing were not to be found in the UK. My first mistake was to work with a bunch of cowboys who were establishing a rehabilitation centre. When I realized what they were up to, the matron and I left on the same day.

'When I later became founding director of a medical charity, the entrepreneurial side of me enjoyed that very much, but the experience was marred by the macho power games always going on. There was only one woman on the board, and there were many conflicts of interests. It is a myth that charity trustees are driven only by altruism. Aware of a crying need for specialists who understand the voluntary sector, two colleagues and I set up a consultancy which offers advice to charities on strategic planning, marketing, trustee selection, training and forth. I did this for three years and am still actively involved, but I missed the hands-on operational side of work and decided to return to being a charity director. In 1995 I was recruited to head up the British Vascular Foundation. Raising funds, launching appeals and so forth – all these involve my skills as a businesswoman and marketing professional.'

Lack of career guidance and career goals

What goals? All too often, at the beginning of their working lives, women have not set themselves clear goals; or, in the case of many women over the past three decades, 'did not recognize I was setting out on a career'. Although the situation has improved over the last ten years, I still hear many women talking about their schools and the expectations (or lack of them) for the female pupils. The family environment and the school careers advice often reinforced the idea that some kind of professional training (nursing, secretarial, teaching), or perhaps university, would be followed by marriage, homemaking and motherhood as sure as night follows day. What was rare was the chance to look beyond that scenario and consider the different options, including following a life-long career, of not necessarily getting married, of possibly not having children, of changing track if the first choice didn't work out, or of pursuing several different types of employment.

The paradox here is that in the 1960s and 1970s, when this attitude was still prevalent, there were plenty of jobs for everyone. As Beverley points out, 'One of the most significant changes from when I was at school and the present day is that we knew we could get a job. That doesn't happen now.'

Theresa went to 'a wonderful girls' school where everyone assumed you would all do very well – which usually meant working for a few years, marrying and having children. If you were outrageously clever, you might carry on doing something as long as the children didn't suffer. I knew of only one woman who went out to work. She was something in the Treasury and this was much derided. It probably meant that the children didn't have puddings during the week!' Theresa also talks about the conflicting assumptions made by the school and the outside world. 'Until I was sixteen I was under the delusion that you set your sights on Cambridge or somewhere like that, but I was told that Cambridge was not the sort of place that girls went to. It was full of boys and not right for girls. That was the prevailing wisdom and before I heard that it had never crossed my mind that boys and girls were treated differently'.

Julia was privately educated in the 1970s at a school

which assumed that women would have a career, and university was both expected and encouraged. Paradoxically, it was Oxford which let her down. She found the University and the Career advisers to be of virtually no help in offering her guidance about what she should do after her degree.

Alison, on the other hand, also privately educated, fared differently again. She found that her school had few expectations for its pupils beyond working as a secretary, teacher or nurse and waiting for Mr Right to come along.

Women who went to mixed-sex schools reported on different experiences. One woman mentioned that she was fortunate enough to be one of seven particularly bright girls in her year and they were encouraged to perform well in class and in exams. She is not so sure that the same would have happened if she had been the only girl with academic aspirations in her form.

Another talked of being very competitive and sporty when at a mixed school and about how she was more likely to be found playing hockey with the boys than netball with the girls. This was frowned upon by the staff and she had to work extra hard to be allowed to enjoy the things she wanted to do as opposed to the things that others thought she ought to do.

Nearly all the women I spoke to mentioned the lack of a range of possibilities offered to them by careers advisers. Sarah who, against great difficulties, did well in her O and A levels, looks back with disappointment at the advice she was given. 'No one ever mentioned PR to me. I also wish that someone had suggested being a magazine editor – I would have loved to have aimed for that.'

The lack of appropriate career guidance at school is still cited as one of the most common obstacles to making the most appropriate job choice for the future, although the service does seem to be improving in some schools. The Institute of Management's 1997 report (*A Question of Balance* – see page 159) found that 25% of the managers in the survey felt that their careers had been hindered in some way by a lack of appropriate guidance. When young people are faced with making important, life-shaping decisions about their futures, the range of choices must seem over-whelming. Well-known and recognized job titles, professions, trades and industries are joined by a whole host of other options which are not so familiar and about which little information is given. But, with the increasing use of computer-based questionnaires to help students find out more about their strengths and weaknesses and to point them in the direction of possible careers and, with easy access to databases, it is now comparatively simple to discover which subjects they need to study to follow a particular interest.

It is not difficult to find out which universities and colleges have the best reputations for specific subjects, or how the relevant courses and their faculties differ from one another. Inevitably, however, there is a limit to the depth of available information and students are often unaware of the entire range of possibilities offered by their preferred subjects. Because of this they are not always able to choose the most appropriate courses, or the ones which would suit them best. It seems to me that the present, rather limited approach to careers guidance is not helpful, particularly now when the possibilities of pursuing a job for life are not high.

The world of work is changing very quickly – much more rapidly than most adults from the conventional world of the professions and nine to five jobs realize. The traditional concept of a 'career' is disappearing and many representatives of the present and future student generations are more than likely to change direction several times during their working lives. The idea of a portfolio career – not relying on one single area of work or skill to generate income – is growing in popularity: especially when employees no longer feel they can rely on a company to provide them with the security that used to be seen as an employer's duty to the workforce. Changes in companies' policies which lead to redundancies or redeployment of resources mean that people are becoming used to the idea of additional training or re-training in order to fill another position within the organization or to find work elsewhere. This will become quite normal and the people who will fare best in an unstable job market are those who learn to be flexible and who develop a range of skills, knowledge and experience.

To this end, career consultants are beginning to emerge who offer a complementary service which can be used alongside the more traditional mechanical approach and which begins the process of thinking about the world of work in a new and exciting way. This approach looks at what kind of organizations the students want to work with, what kind of lifestyle they aspire to, and how they will measure personal success. It concentrates less on a specific area of work or profession and more on what the individual student hopes to give to and receive from his or her working life. Students can then begin to clarify the direction they wish to follow and also take the chance to research and explore the various possibilities that open up to them.

If young people were offered an improved careers guidance service, then I'm sure that it would not be so common to hear adults making dissatisfied comments, such as:

'My career has tended to follow the path of opportunity rather than any clearly defined strategy', or

'. . . late discovery of what I wanted to do and late discovery of my talents.'

It is interesting to look at the two apparently conflicting meanings of the word 'career'. As a noun, it implies the existence of a systematic path through your working life. As a verb, it expresses rushing about without any apparent focus. Which definition do you follow? Do you see a case for changing from one to the other? It would seem from these two definitions that each of us can make a considered choice about the next step in our lives – at whatever point it occurs.

This is not to say that everyone needs, or is suited to a clearly defined career path, but it does seem obvious to me that some of the wasted time and talent evident in many women's early lives could be avoided with a more thorough and knowledgeable approach to career counselling from the outset.

The same principle applies later on. For example, one manager talked of:

> 'Not having clear goals in the sense of promotion,
> failing to recognize opportunities for advancement, not
> reading how the system worked.'

Traditionally, the idea of designing your future in terms of work was more likely to be found among the boys than the girls and this is recognized by women managers:

> 'I was probably less focused upon my career goals than
> my male counterparts. I was more concerned with job
> *achievement* than job *progression*.'

Having a limited academic education, or not being educated to degree level, are the two main reasons given by women, who describe themselves as late developers or for lacking confidence in themselves and their professional capabilities.

Case study – Judy

Judy, 43, is married with two young children and is the head of a central support team in a local authority. She has a degree in business studies and also trained as a barrister. She is a non-executive director of an NHS Trust.

'No one in my family had been to university before – they had not even thought about it – but when I realized that university was a prospect for me I was encouraged by an uncle. Money was a problem, so I was driven to aim for a university degree with sponsorship funding. My father had been a shop manager, so business was seen as highly respectable and going into business was seen as a good idea. As I was female and good with people, Personnel seemed to be the obvious route to everyone else. BP offered me a sponsorship and I accepted a four-year 'thin sandwich' course, with a salary on graduation which was more than my father's. From then on my feet didn't touch the ground. I moved every six months, including a stint working in Scotland on the North Sea operation.

'I obtained a good degree and specialized in Industrial Relations and Employment Law. I thought about professional qualifications and, because I had done well at law, the lecturer suggested I went for the Bar which I had never even contemplated. "Why not?" I needed to try. My father advised me, "Never regret anything", so I applied and got in – but most of my family thought I was crazy. My husband liked to show off about my aspirations to become a barrister, but he didn't like my studying. After graduating, I moved to UK Oil to work in personnel-related research, and Industrial Relations which I really enjoyed. Around the same time, I was called to the Bar. The respect I found I was being shown at work served to reinforce what I was beginning to feel about myself – which was counter to what was happening at home. I left the house and my marriage and never looked back. In 1980, when I was twenty-six, my first case was my own divorce.

'After I qualified, I soon realized that there were too many barristers on the market and, anyway, I knew I wanted the chance to apply my legal knowledge on a practical level and decided to remain in industry. The opportunity arose to apply for the job of Personnel Officer at the company's research centre and later as the Training Officer for the whole site, comprising 2000 people. I now had to put into practice what I had learned in theory and I found myself in one of the most satisfying jobs I have ever had. I consolidated my own life, bought my own flat and became financially independent. Simultaneously, my relationship with an ex-colleague had become particularly special and in 1984 we decided to make it official. We had both been through divorces and the stress of this had opened up for me a sideline interest in complementary medicine, starting with reflexology.

'"Where next?" As a lawyer, my obvious choice should have been the legal department. I enquired about the possibility of getting a commercial pupillage, but that didn't materialize and I took the commercial lawyer's post. Experience quickly showed that, while I was capable of doing the job, I did not fit in with the stereotype. When I tried to make changes, I was totally ignored and concluded that this job was not for me when one of my previous managers asked me directly why I was there – and I couldn't answer. He asked me to join him in management training.

'The two years had not been fulfilling as a job, but we had a lot to sort out on the personal side. My husband, David, moved first to Hampshire and then to Kent, so I was commuting long distance *and* managing three homes! By now I was expecting our first child and suddenly, in 1986, everything was starting to come together. A group of us devised the Integrated MBA and teamed up with Warwick Business School as our academic partner. We also formed a Business School Network with British Airways and offered back critique to the business schools.

'I was beginning to experience problems with a boss who was finding my innovative approach both disconcerting and a threat. I realized that I had found the glass ceiling in this organization and decided to move on. The choice was either to take up a senior post with my local county council, or to go out on my own. I decided I needed more experience before I became a consultant, so I applied for the education job. I knew that financially it could be a major problem, but also that I would never be given the same level of responsibility in the old job. It would mean a huge drop in salary, loss of an interest-free loan, car and so on. Coincidentally, the *Economist* had been writing reports on MBAs and asked me to be their adviser. They also required an author for their report, *Guide to Executive Programmes in Europe and the USA* and I offered to do it. The payment was exactly the sum I needed to make up the shortfall in salary so I resigned – BP was stunned that I should leave after seventeen years. They made a counter offer, but I knew I had to go to the new job where I would be in charge of many more people and have greater responsibility. I also felt that BP's professional standards had declined and that, if I did not act, they would compromise my own standards.

'There were huge differences between the two jobs, especially resources, the things you take for granted – no secretaries, little support, money being tight. The management structure largely comprised ex-teachers, many of whom I came to realize were entrenched in individuality and chauvinism – "teacher always knows best". As the majority of those in charge were men, it was inevitable that the culture was dominated by macho attitudes, far worse than those of any oil company. Local management was being introduced and it was my job to help the transition. We felt the pressures of devolution and how it affects people if they are not handled in the right way. We were there to help them, and the challenge I enjoyed was putting together a team from a very mixed bunch of people with diverse backgrounds and strengths. People were expecting results from us, which they could show off about, but it was soon clear that the fundamentals – the essential building blocks such as sound contracts, efficient and effective information systems – did not exist. With the first wave of capping and budget cuts, I managed one of the biggest redundancy exercises they had ever had to face in a seventeen-union setting. I was now expecting my second baby. It was a time of considerable stress – not helped by the lack of support from the people above me and not enough people to do the work required. I knew I couldn't do any more and I urged them to replace me while I was on maternity leave with someone from the central team and one male assistant director agreed to do it. It opened his eyes to what it had been like for me. The personnel director said he would like me to work with him and so it was agreed that, when I returned, I would manage one of five corporate projects involving management development. I ended up with all five! One of the department's main achievements was devising a rolling programme called 'Making Connections', which covered more than 1200 managers. We won a local government award for excellence and parts of the programme still exist today.

'When I moved to the head office, my colleagues were not expecting too much (although I didn't realize it at the time), but it turned out to be a great success. I was free to network and to create – activities which I know are essential to my sanity and my health. When my director became deputy chief executive, I was appointed his personal adviser and, after a period of reorganization, I negotiated to manage a multi-functional team. This was 1992–3.

'Initially I was the only woman on the management team of ten and the men candidly asked, "Can we trust you?". We've since developed a good relationship based on trust and mutual respect. It's interesting that several directors developed posts similar to mine in their own departments – in all cases held by senior women managers. We act as catalysts, mediators, a conscience – part of the Yin and Yang balance. Watching the effectiveness of these male/female partnerships has confirmed my view that organizations need a mind, a body and a spirit – and a healthy male/female management balance enables you to achieve this if they are equal partners.

'My husband retired early at the time I was going back to work. He joined the board of governors of a school, was appointed as an industrial tribunal member and has become more involved in the local community. He's now able to give more time to the family and to enjoy the children as they grow up.

'I've been courted by headhunters to return to the private sector, but none of the offers have felt right and I know my current position is enabling me to gain the kind of experience difficult to match anywhere else. Within the last three months, I have been appointed a non-executive director of a local NHS Trust. It is work that I enjoy immensely and it complements my full-time role with the Council.'

Family pressures and expectations

Older women often cite the traditional attitudes towards girls and work, which prevailed during their teenage years, as an obstacle to their pursuit of a career at that time. Often families were disinterested in supporting the type of higher education – financially, or otherwise – which would have helped girls as they started their working lives. Many women, particularly those over forty, mention being almost brainwashed by their mothers saying that you couldn't combine a family and career. They talk of a little voice whispering in their ears, reminding them of the detrimental effects it would have on everyone involved. Families, often with the best of motives, can have a profound and unhelpful effect on girls' decisions about their futures, and common to the experience of all these women is the memory of always being told by other people of what they *should* do.

Beverley would have liked to have been a policewoman. Her father didn't think that would be a good idea because he thought she would be too lenient and so she studied hotel and catering instead. As it turned out, this was the wrong choice for her, too. 'I think I felt that that sort of life would be interesting because of the variety. I actually discovered that I was to become a jack of all trades and master of none. Enjoyable as the course was, at the end of it you weren't trained as anything in particular'.

Families may also continue to hinder the progress of women family members throughout their working lives. I was sorry, but not surprised, to hear recently of one young woman who was having to take a great deal of time off work because her mother was unwell. When her employer found out that she lived at home with her parents and four brothers, he asked why it always fell to her to look after the sick mother. It hadn't occurred to the young woman, her mother, father or brothers that it could be any other way.

For women who have a partner and children, the main issue is what one manager calls 'multi-priority juggling'. If there is little or no help at home and only grudging support for the woman, the whole business of trying to sustain a relationship, bring up children, maintain a home and follow a career is daunting. In the relatively few, but increasing number of cases where the woman is the sole breadwinner for the family, it is almost impossible for her to contemplate further full-time education, for example, if that is what she needs to make up for any previous lack of academic achievement. Career breaks – in particular, maternity leave – may also lead to a temporary halt in a manager's progress and this results in, again, women's full and effective membership of a management team being rather later than their male colleagues.

Juggling the varied aspects of a home and working life does not necessarily become any easier when there are no children involved – though of course, this affects working couples with young families too:

> 'What I've found difficult is the choice and subsequent need from the start of my career to balance the needs of marriage, separate careers and later family responsibilities to ageing parents.'

The issue of elderly dependants is a growing one. In the Institute of Management's 1997 survey of managers' changing professional and personal values (*A Question of Balance* – see page 159), the point was made that flexible working policies developed by family-friendly employers have largely concentrated on childcare. Nearly half of the female respondents to the survey indicated that help with the care of elderly dependants was an important issue for them.

There are many different ways in which discouragement or obstructive behaviour, within a family structure or relationship, makes it very difficult for women to follow their chosen career paths. It is not easy, for instance, for those women embroiled in domestic violence to escape. One manager said that it had taken her a long time to get out of such a situation and she had chosen to tread water for a while as her work was the only fixed point in her life. The positive outcome of all this was that she learned to be strong inside.

A successful professional woman who is now a partner in her own business describes how obstructive her husband has been:

> 'He disliked the idea of me becoming financially independent and regarded my career as unimportant. He has consistently put as many obstacles in my way as he could and has no interest in the company, unless

I say that we are in the red – in which case he tells me that the whole venture has been a waste of time and effort!'

In addition, the media coverage of women who 'have made it' has been the subject of some criticism, which suggests that too much emphasis is given to domestic and family background rather than to their business achievements. The inevitable concentration by journalists on questions such as, 'How does she cope with a high-profile career *and* running a family?' often contrasts with profiles of businessmen, where details of whether or not they are married, or how many children he has, are omitted.

Case study – Carol

Carol 39, is a lone parent with two young children. She is a quality adviser in financial services.

'I wanted to be a physiotherapist, but the career counsellor told me that I would need chemistry A level and that there was no way I would pass that. Four years later I found out this was not true. This was 1974 and I had four O levels. My father suggested I became a programmer and, because I didn't know what else to do, I went to Vauxhalls as an apprentice. I was lucky to get the apprenticeship – my father must have recognized a latent skill. Vauxhalls gave me a superb grounding – they trained their employees in the whole business, so that you knew what the impact was of your individual job. Later I was able to apply my common sense in other companies; it helped me to see the whole picture much more than others who had been only theory based. In one job I was almost sacked when Personnel dis-covered I hadn't got a degree, but my boss said he wanted to keep me because I could do the job. I contracted for a while, but I didn't like that because I didn't feel I belonged.

'I ended up at Hewlett-Packard which was brilliant. I travelled to Geneva and California – I had a wonderful time. By now I was twenty-six and a senior analyst/team leader. My programming background meant I could relate to the programmers and I saw my role as supporting them.

'I left Hewlett-Packard when I was pregnant because at the time they didn't employ anyone on a part-time basis and I didn't want to work full time. We moved to Bristol, but I split up with my husband, and I ended up working full time with two children to look after.

'If I had stayed with Hewlett-Packard, I would probably have remained in IT and would not have moved to my current job in a financial services company. My development here started when somebody said, "If you keep your head down, you'll be fine". I nearly died at that! All I kept hearing was, "This is the way we do things here" and I knew that it was wrong. My work and my marriage were going along the same lines. I kept thinking, "If I give in, I will lose me and I'm worth more than that". I fought and fought. At last, my husband and I separated and things also changed at work with the arrival of a new general manager. He really stirred us all up and made us believe in empowerment for everyone. With some outside consultants he introduced an organization development programme which involved every single employee and I became deeply involved in that.

'At the moment, my children are the most important thing in my life and my time and money are tied up with them. As long as I am still learning and meeting challenges in my job, that's OK for the next eleven years. I don't want to be shouting at the children all the time because I'm stressed out. I don't want work to need me more than they do.

'I will never stop learning. It helps you relate to the human race – especially children. It's so easy to forget what it's like to not know "everything". It keeps you young and helps keep things in perspective.'

Personal limitations

High on the list of obstacles for an astonishing number of working women comes an absence of self-confidence and a lack of belief in their own abilities. Many women never push themselves forward – often because they've been brought up to believe that this is not acceptable 'feminine' behaviour, and because they don't appreciate that playing to their strengths and abilities in an assertive rather than aggressive way will invariably command respect and inspire confidence in both men and women alike. They don't recognize the need to understand internal company politics and often express disapproval at the 'macho' way in which business is conducted and refuse to participate. Sometimes they find themselves in a situation where, even if they don't appreciate their own talents, less qualified or experienced male colleagues find them threatening. This often occurs when they are seen to be challenging the status quo, having identified that the 'accepted way of doing things', i.e. the culture of an organization, is not always the most comfortable within which to work. This position naturally leads to a complete breakdown in communication and an inability to work together effectively. Women who lack belief in their own capabilities also give examples of being interrupted and talked over – even when they've been asked to give an opinion based on their expertise – *and letting it happen*.

The tendency of some women to underestimate their skills, not to reach their full potential, and the failure to grasp opportunities has been acknowledged as a characteristic which correlates directly to a lack of fulfilment and a realization that women managers are not always being true to themselves. It is common to hear women managers saying, 'No one was more surprised than I was when I got the job', or 'My c.v. looked so good I could hardly believe it was mine', or 'I seem to be coping all right – I only hope it lasts'. The good news is that women are finally beginning to learn from *all* their experiences.

Theresa's unusual and varied early, working life gave her plenty of opportunity to learn about running a business and managing people, but it was not until she was thirty-nine that she understood quite how much she knew and could offer an employer – in particular, her ability to visualize how the various parts of an organization interconnect.

Sarah was actually aware early on that education would be the key to her success and, against the odds, continued at school and went on to study at university. Having graduated, she embarked upon several fulfilling jobs, but they provided her, however, with a set of skills which were to prove invaluable when she started to build on her interest in PR and the emerging area of IT. She also knew how to grasp an opportunity when it arose. 'I have been lucky with my timing. I was around just when PCs were coming to the fore and I was interested in the product. Some of the firms I worked for were still stuck in the 1980s – hard and chauvinistic – and had awful management styles. I learned what I could from them and also saw what I didn't want to copy.'

Zoë knows that she has had a lot of opportunities, 'mostly because people knew I would get the job done and partly to give me the chance to do different things'. She also concedes, however, that in the past she tried to keep everyone happy, and 'the more I thought about the impact of my behaviour on others in the workplace, the more disempowering for me work became and the less clear I was of what I did think'. She is consciously pursuing her need to be truer to herself at work 'to say what I think, rather than what will get me promoted and to behave in ways which *I* think are appropriate rather than what I perceive the organizations thinks is right'.

Where women recognize that both overt and covert rules exist within organizations, but refuse to 'play it by the book', and either make the rules up for themselves or modify them to their advantage, they can introduce significant changes.

For instance, when Theresa was asked to set up an audiovisual unit and to provide material for courses in a management college, she introduced learning materials which incorporated a range of subject matter. 'The internal people found it threatening because it was a challenge to the accepted way of doing things and meant that the lecturer was no longer king.' It is interesting that, while the students and participants benefited enormously from her innovative approach, Theresa found that she was having to win influence within the company ranks by getting approval from outside the organization and bringing it back inside. Theresa has even used examples from her early working life as the basis for case studies in her management college.

It is not always easy to detect the factors which have helped or hindered your career, especially when you are following a path of particular interest. One woman, trained as a lawyer, who worked in the Civil Service for many years but left to become a consultant, was an active advocate of equal opportunities and worked tirelessly for the cause of women managers, especially during the 1970s. She comments wryly that this work *may* have furthered her career, but she rather doubts it!

One of the exciting aspects of talking to successful women managers is listening to how they have recognized opportunities when they arose, how they have learnt from past experiences and how they have coped with changing circumstances. This theme is summarized by Alison's query, 'Is the rest of my life going to be like this?', or Carol's realization when both her work and her marriage were not going well, 'If I give in, I will lose me and I'm worth more than that'.

During the early part of their working lives, all my interviewees gained invaluable experience of how *not* to run a business and how *not* to deal with people, as well as learning the basic management and technical skills which have formed the basis of their careers to date. They felt particularly uncomfortable with the confrontational stance often adopted by male colleagues and with the tendency to shout down opposing views without considering their merits. The personal touch favoured by women may lead to difficulties with those male managers who prefer an arms-length relationship with their staff and colleagues.

For the current generation of school leavers, the reality of their career expectations may sit uneasily with the expectations of their parents who grew up in a very different world of 'jobs for life'. Perhaps parents, too, need some assistance in accepting the major changes that have taken place. As successful women managers bring up their own children, or have influence over nieces, nephews, godchildren and other young people, they will have a significant role to play in ensuring that informed advice is passed on. A strong sense of optimism exists that the daughters of current women managers will not tolerate the degree of pressure that their mothers have had to endure in trying to maintain a balanced life and will continue to influence the changes in corporate culture.

ACTION PLAN:

1 Think carefully about your personal objectives for both your career and other aspects of your life and make certain they will enable you to maintain a balance between work and home commitments.
2 Make sure you receive good careers advice which is tailored to your individual objectives, aspirations and interests, and which does not try to force you into a direction you don't feel comfortable with.
3 Discuss career choices and issues with members of your

family (and other friends whose opinion you value), but don't give in to pressure unless you fully agree with their views.

4 Don't underestimate your skills and qualities, or dismiss any previous experiences and knowledge as irrelevant – knowledge is never wasted.

5 Be organized and determined in your approach to realizing your ambitions. Try to think beyond your perceived limitations and make the effort to recognize and seize all available opportunities.

6 Don't be afraid to re-assess your objectives from time to time as your circumstances change.

HELP IS AT HAND

People naturally look to others with either the same background or with whom they have some shared experience to help in times of uncertainty and women usually expect support and help from other women. However, even though the culture of male-dominated organizations and the attitudes of male managers have been the most frequent obstacles that women managers have had to overcome, it seems that other women do not usually play a larger part than men in helping female managers build their self-confidence and in encouraging them to progress within their chosen line of work. While there is much talk about the need for women role models, there seem to be precious few examples of them. One of the recurrent themes in discussion with women managers is the lack of high-profile, senior, successful women who offer encouragement to others or provide evidence of what can be achieved. The handful, whose names immediately spring to mind, are inundated with requests for interviews, lectures and so on and, quite reasonably, feel rather overwhelmed by the attention and sometimes resentful of the time it takes to fulfil these engagements. They would surely welcome the appearance of more women on the scene to spread the burden and the gospel?

The encouraging news is that, at last, there are more women around who are prepared to talk about how they have reached and maintained high office and who are happy to discuss the reasons for their success. There is a feeling that those older women – who made their way to the top fighting and scratching and weren't willing to assist others – are a disappearing breed and that the new generation is more amenable to lending a helping hand.

Even if they haven't been seen to help directly, women managers often do so indirectly, just by being there, by listening, perhaps by providing the instant 'camaraderie' of being another woman in a predominantly male meeting.

Case study – Beverley
Beverley, 42, is married with two children, and until recently, worked as a commissioning manager in a health authority. She has since moved internally into a more strategic role in primary care. She has a BSc (Hotel and Catering) and a diploma in Management Studies (DMS).

'I wanted to be a policeman or forensic scientist, but my father said I was too soft. My headmistress thought I should go into horticulture, but I hated anything to do with plants. It's strange she should have said that because, over the past twenty years, I've spent a lot of time in my garden.

'I chose a Hotel and Catering course because of the variety that I thought there would be, but I discovered that I became a jack of all trades and master of none. I had an exchange year in the States and did an industry year in one of the London hotels in the Rank Group. I got on well with everyone and at the end they found me a job in my local Rank hotel. That proved a problem because the general manager there always thought that I hadn't got there through the proper procedures, that I had been imposed on him. This was 1977. I didn't last very long – we were working very long hours for very little money, so I left.

'When I applied for a job at the City Council, they asked me what I hated doing most and I told them maths and figures. They inquired about what kind of people I didn't like working with and I told them people who waste their talent and time. I ended up doing figures for three days a week and working with people who were bone idle. I was meant to be doing Work Study, but I finally left because I didn't think I was being stretched at all.

'It was 1979 when I went into the NHS for the first time. I became a personnel assistant in the district HQ, specializing in health and safety, trades union negotiation, and in charge of looking after the community staff. I did a good, basic course in first-line management and after fifteen months moved to a small cottage hospital, where I dealt with all the day-to-day problems which occur in the real world of managing people and dealing with sick people. At the next health service reorganization, I was promoted and joined another hospital as deputy unit administrator. My male boss encouraged me a lot and sent me on day release to do a Diploma in Management Studies. The networks were good and there was a feeling of co-operation. I left full-time work in 1985 when I became pregnant and, when I returned to full-time work in 1992, the attitudes I found to women in the workplace were very different.

'After the birth of my first child, I worked part time for the Community Unit until my husband lost his job. We ran a nursery and landscaping business for three years from my mother-in-law's house. The business did well, but when I became pregnant again we had to make a decision about continuing the nursery and buying the house. We decided not to buy the house, but to renovate a wreck whilst living in a caravan and coping with two small children.

'I continued with some part-time work for the NHS, mostly in the evenings, but we were getting into financial difficulty because my husband couldn't find anything permanent. I talked to him about my going back full time with him looking after the children and, when he agreed, I rang one of my NHS contacts who let me know about suitable vacancies. I became contracts manager, which included negotiating with the fundholders and health authorities. In 1984, when I didn't get an expected promotion, I moved to the FHSA (Family Health Support Agency) who had headhunted me. It was a difficult time, especially when the FHSA merged with the health authority and the people in charge didn't recognize the opportunity for growth and development. During the reorganization, I joined the neighbouring authority. I'm well paid, I like my colleagues, I get on well with my local Provider Trust, and I find my job challenging.

'If I had to do everything over again, I would recommend a profession – something to hang your hat on – because administrators are rarely valued for what they are. If you listen to Radio 4 and hear all the time that hospital administrators are overpaid and useless, you begin to believe it.'

Colleagues

One's first experience of working for a manager clearly makes a lasting impression. Many women realize that some of the people they worked with and for were examples of how *not* to manage an organization and the people within it. Being aware of this proves to be almost as valuable as learning how to work effectively in partnership with colleagues and how to be organized and manage one's own workload. Colleagues have an important and formative part to play at work, yet managers do not always appreciate how much they can gain by asking for help and support from their peers. Senior management are not always aware of the positive contribution that they can make to an employee's feeling of inclusion into their work team, department or organization. The culture of an organization has a significant impact on the extent to which people feel part of the team – which in turn determines how well they work together. It is therefore a key aspect of the managerial role that new colleagues are effectively inducted and in this position women managers could help a great deal by setting an appropriate tone for their workgroups.

Two different comments illustrate how women's experience of encouragement and guidance at work can vary from one end of the spectrum to the other:

> 'Some supervisors and managers were helpful while I was being trained. Once I gained management status, this assistance stopped.'

But on the other hand,

> 'The only help I have received has been since I became successful.'

Learning about diversity from colleagues has also proved an invaluable management lesson:

> 'My current line manager has shown me the advantages of a completely different management style from my own and got me thinking about the importance of difference.'

Judy benefited from the experience of help and support from one of her department's long-term managers when she was working in Scotland, far away from parents and friends. He coached her, tested her to her full potential and did everything he could to foster her development. She was also assisted by her law lecturer at college, when she was considering professional qualifications, who suggested that she try for the Bar. She had never even contemplated such a career move and his encouragement led her to apply, study and eventually be called to the Bar.

In organizations where there are senior women managers, they tend to be supportive and encouraging of their junior colleagues. As mentioned earlier, this is a move away from the attitudes shown by some successful women in past decades. Typical of the support given is:

> 'I had a woman manager who gave me almost unlimited opportunities for development through allowing me to try new things.'

> 'My manager arranged supervision sessions with members of a university faculty to clarify goals and to provide challenge and support to situations faced at work. She also helped me to understand personal and organizational needs within our department.'

One woman who went through a particularly difficult domestic crisis remembers:

> 'One of my managers was flexible at a time of lengthy illness and, as long as I did the work well, he didn't mind when or where I did it. Some men have been very good at caring.'

Sarah interprets the idea of assistance from colleagues to include the support she has received from her first account. 'They have stayed with me and given me the backing I need. They put us on the map and, as the work has grown, it has become a long-term partnership. The managers are supportive of my work and they have almost become business advisers to me – willing to discuss matters if I have any problems in running my business.' She cites this example in direct contrast to the behaviour of the new generation of bank managers, who she feels 'are only interested in covering their backsides. The old-fashioned bank managers took an interest, knew you as a person. The problem, today, for small businesses is that there is not enough encouragement, particularly from the banks. It is hard work all the way.'

Family

For men and women alike, family members play a vital role in providing the necessary support and encouragement needed to achieve a healthy balance between a successful and rewarding career and a happy and fulfilling life outside of the office.

For women managers, family – when combined with help from colleagues – is of particular importance: it enables women managers to operate on an equal footing with their male counterparts. Parents, partners and children who not only show their approval, but are interested, too, are seen as a real advantage if women are to succeed at work.

Zoë acknowledges that 'my husband has always encouraged me when I lacked confidence and, as my children have grown up, they have given invaluable help not only by their support for my ideas but by challenging me and making me think things through.'

Julia's husband is in the army, but mostly they have been based in London which has been lucky. 'There is no "competition" between us in the sense of jobs. He is incredibly supportive and it must be really difficult if you don't have that assistance and the willingness to join in with the nappy changing and so on.'

Role Models, Coaches and Mentors

It is worth looking at the differences between these three capacities as there is a tendency to talk about them as if they were the same thing.

Role models

It seems to me that the concept of 'role model' has been so liberally applied that it is beginning to lose some of its original meaning. By definition, it refers to an individual that you would wish to be like in a *specific* aspect, not necessarily in every way. For example, the female leader of a local council, which has survived and even thrived on the major upheavals of the past four years, is generally acknowledged as having achieved significant results both for the town and for the council employees. Yet, when asked about being a role model for other women, she laughs and suggests that her domestic arrangements are unusual enough not to be considered an appropriate example, but she does admit that what she has achieved at work is something to be proud of, something that she is happy to discuss. If you are inspired by someone else's approach to work, you can choose that as one aspect of behaviour you wish to emulate in your own job.

Coaches

Coaches aid individuals to develop specific attitudes, knowledge and skills. Strictly speaking it is a line manager's role to act as a coach, to bring people up to their level of competence required to do their job. Sadly, until recently, it was rarely built into line managers' job specifications that they should undergo training in coaching and that their mastery of coaching be included in their appraisals. Increasingly at senior level, coaching is being outsourced and the resulting conversations are highly confidential with no reporting back to line managers. There are several different types of external coaches, including specialist consultants and sport personalities – who have developed their skills in strategy, team building and motivation and transferred them from the sports field into the workplace.

One of the most frequently used sources of coaching seems to be the outside consultants. There are numerous examples of consultants, or trainers, who have been hired to work on a particular project within an organization and who have, over time, become a confidant(e) to whom a manager can turn and discuss a wide range of issues. In one predominantly-male organization, a woman manager noted, 'Usually the female influences are not within the company, but come from other women working as consultants who are therefore independent of corporate pressures'. This relationship continues long after the official contract with the organization has ended. One manager talks of 'gaining very helpful personal executive coaching which still continues on an *ad hoc* basis'.

Outside consultants can be extremely influential: as both Theresa and Carol discovered after working alongside consultants who came to work within their organizations. Carol knew instinctively that she was both fair and intuitive in her approach to her colleagues and the way they worked, but felt that her actions were often blocked by more senior managers. She was aware that others had written her off because she didn't have a degree, would volunteer for everything and would question anything she didn't understand or agree with. 'Some outside consultants came in to work with us on a change programme. Until then, it was all gut feeling with me. I didn't have the right language and it was very frustrating. I hadn't had any training and then these consultants told me what was happening. I talked to them, I went on training courses, I ran some communications workshops, and I then had the language to analyse what had happened and to know that I had been right all along.'

When Theresa joined her organization's Business Development department one of her successes involved helping to run an advanced management programme with an outside consultant. 'I was apprehensive about what the consultant would think about me, but he was wise enough not to mind and the whole exercise marked the beginning of a new phase in my working life when I began to have fun again.'

The more senior the manager, the greater the need to ensure that his or her own thinking and ideas are tested by a detached, but empathetic and experienced, person. Managers and directors at the top of organizations often feel isolated and there are few other people around at the same level with whom it is possible, or even desirable, to discuss uncertainties or thoughts for the future, and an outside coach can prove an invaluable source of inspiration and clarity.

Mentors

Traditionally, senior internal employees have acted as mentors to more junior individuals, providing them with advice on how best to steer their career through an organization. However, reengineering and down-sizing over the last few years has resulted in the sacking of many older people in organizations and as a result it has become more difficult to find an appropriate senior manager to fill that niche – so in many cases what used to be an internal role is now becoming an external role. The individual may, therefore, choose someone from another organization, another function or a retired person whom they respect to act as their mentor.

Women managers are still feeling their way up the corporate ladder and many say that there is a dearth of appropriate mentors to aid their progress. Historically, mentors have been 'unofficial': that is, they have been experienced contacts who have taken on the role of sounding board or adviser more by chance than design. Yet, there is currently a fashion for appointing 'official' mentors particularly if an organization is experiencing great change, or where managers feel they would benefit from some personal attention as part of their own development.

The importance of having these professional individuals to turn to for a fresh perspective on work-related issues is now recognized in most organizations. Managers often describe them as 'people of high integrity, giving support by creating the environment in which you could perform successfully, and in which you could also make, and admit to mistakes – as long as you learned from them'.

Friend and networks

Individual friends and extended groups of contacts within an industry are particularly useful for the expansion of learning and are often described as being of 'immense value and encouragement'. One manager speaks of 'two or three men who have been really helpful by deliberately introducing me to their network of friends without requiring me to be "one of the boys"'.

Networking is mentioned time and time again as a highly-valued source of support and inspiration. These networks may take several forms. Associations such as City Women's Network, Business and Professional Women and European Women's Development Network Society provide a comprehensive programme of events and services which are geared towards enriching the lives and careers of professional women. Other groups such as the Institute of Personnel and Development, the Association for Management Education and Development, the various bodies representing banking, marketing and management consultants, the Royal Society of Arts and many others, often have separate women's interest groups. (A full list with contact addresses is given at the end of the book.) These, together with the other activities which include professional colleagues of both sexes, provide the necessary balance. Within organizations, informal networks of other senior women frequently exist, which also offer friendship and encouragement. In addition, attending conferences not only broadens these networks, but also makes sure that you keep your name and face in people's minds.

With a group of managers from several organizations who were looking for an MBA programme that would suit their particular needs, Judy devised the Integrated MBA. 'We formed a mutually-beneficial partnership and together established the first competency-based, action-learning-based MBA and chose Warwick Business School as our academic partner. We also formed a Business School Network with British Airways and offered back critique to the business schools. We shared a very special experience and this forged a friendship between all the parties involved which still lasts to this day.'

Networks don't have to be formal arrangements: Theresa, manager of a Management College for a UK clearing bank, talks of 'building relationships with the policymakers and others in Head Office – so when they took over our college for the group we already knew each other well and we could talk about what the college should be doing'.

Beverley has worked within the NHS for several years, but not continuously. She has found the internal network to be extremely effective and when she has wanted to move back into work, or to change jobs, she has been able to call upon her contacts for advice and assistance.

Alison is also a great believer in the power of networking and feels that it plays an invaluable role in shaping and directing her career, especially in light of her own lack of formal management education and training. 'If only I had known at the age of eighteen, or even twelve, that networking is the route to power, support, advice, career opportunities and unlimited professional help. It's a two-way process – you need to give back as well as receive.'

As lack of self-confidence is cited as one of the major blockages to women achieving their goals at work, the thoughtful use of networks is one method of beginning to build self-assurance in a safe and supportive environment. Joining committees, speaking at meetings and representing the network outside the office – all this combines to developing a manager's skills, knowledge and experience, thereby reducing the sense of isolation and instead gradually increasing the feeling of self-esteem and belief in one's capabilities.

Books and Articles

It is, of course, impossible to suggest reading material which will be useful to, or universally appreciated by, all women managers. What is riveting to one person may leave another cold; what inspires one manager may be perceived as trite or 'old hat' to another; a style that stimulates one woman's thinking may infuriate another – what is helpful is a very personal issue.

There is also a distinction between what is beneficial on a professional basis and what assists you as a person. There are times when general, but regular, reading of newspapers, journals and magazines is sufficient to keep up-to-date with regional, national and international affairs. Other occasions call for a more focused, indepth insight into specific subjects.

Some managers, who would describe themselves as self-taught (usually meaning that they have had to develop their careers in isolation), admit that they have not used any books to help them, but now think that perhaps they would have benefited. Another group agrees that constant reading of newspapers and books of all sorts has been important, but their general opinion is that, 'I have not been particularly inspired by management or business writing'. This feeling is not unusual: 'I review current and past literature on a periodic basis, based on my own needs and interests at the time. There are a few that have been helpful, but the proliferation of what I call "tactical" business/career management books are the ones I skim through. I don't find them as sustaining.'

Yet most of the women managers I know read voraciously. Reading business books is seen as one clear way of keeping abreast of new trends and distilling knowledge into an overall perspective of what to do and how to do it. This was summed up by one female manager who said, 'There are so many good things to read. The consistent factor about the most useful books is that they are easy to read, they help me to do my job (the technical side) and they guide my development as a learner in all aspects of my life.'

Some books, authors and other publications are regularly mentioned and they are worth a special note here (in addition to the general booklist at the end of this book):

Harvard Business Review
For many years this has printed articles by many of the leading and acknowledged gurus in the field of management and encourages a rigorous approach to reading and learning.

The Economist
This weekly publication remains one of the most influential and knowledgeable distillations of world news in the English language.

Men are from Mars, Women are from Venus: A Practical Guide For Improving Communication and Getting What You Want in Your Relationships
John Gray (Thorsons)

You Just Don't Understand: Women and Men in Conversation
Deborah Tannen (Virago)
This book shows the differences in the way language is used

by men and women and looks at the reasons for this.

Women Who Run with the Wolves: Contacting the Power of the Wild Woman
Clarissa Pinkola Estés (Rider)
The author argues that woman's genuine nature has been repressed for centuries by a value system that trivializes emotional truth, intuitive wisdom and instinctual self-confidence. She draws on a wide range of myths and stories to teach women how they can reclaim and rejoice in their true feminine power.

The Influential Woman: How to Achieve Success in Your Career – and Still Enjoy Your Personal Life:
Lee Bryce (Piatkus)
In looking at what holds women back from reaching senior positions, Lee Bryce offers both analysis and practical advice and describes a female model of power and success.

Courses and outside activities

As with publications, the value of training and development programmes depends on several aspects, in particular the requirements of the participants and the quality of the tutors and materials involved.

Many organizations arrange their own training and development programmes and some business sectors are particularly adept at covering a wide range of topics extremely successfully. For example, managers from several different areas within the NHS have mentioned the availability of in-house courses such as Developing Change Resources, Accelerated Development Programme, Leading Change in the Public Sector, Training for Trainers, Course for Experienced Personnel Officers and a whole host of alternative internal activities which are aimed at encouraging team working, personal effectiveness and other management skills. The NHS also run a number of women-only initiatives.

Other activities or areas of training, perhaps not directly a part of the job, might also be applicable and may perhaps contribute to the confidence-building exercise. Managers' original disciplines, even if not wholly relevant now, sometimes comprise elements which are applicable to current jobs. This is often where outside interests often come in useful. One manager speaks of her training in bereavement counselling. 'Alongside my job I work with the dying and bereaved in a hospice – some real transferable life skills here!'. On another level, image consultants have been particularly helpful to those of us who are not innately chic to knock our wardrobes into some semblance of order and suitability – so that we may feel confident that what we wear at work reflects a mixture of our personality and capability.

Women are capable of making the same impact at work as men. However, women need to be confident of their abilities, assured in their methods of making sure they are heard and noticed and dogged in their efforts to push themselves forward. 'Women need to prepare themselves thoroughly to be taken seriously and that means dress, speech, etc as well as skills and knowledge. They must invest time and money to broaden their horizons. I'm always saddened when I hear women say they can't or won't spend money on training and development and their wardrobes'.

It is clear that help, support and encouragement for women in pursuit of their career goals can come from a wide range of sources, not necessarily just from other women. Most would welcome greater interaction with the women who have reached the top – so that they can gain confidence by their example and believe that they are capable of similar achievements, and that it is worth aiming for. This issue emerged as one of the most heartfelt and pressing as far as women managers are concerned.

ACTION PLAN:

1 Seek out women who you admire – family friends, teachers, colleagues at any level in the organization, social contacts or managers from other companies – and talk to them about their career paths and your aspirations.

2 When the time is appropriate, ask a woman you respect to take on the informal role of mentor – someone to whom you can turn when you have issues to discuss.

3 Make sure that partners and, where relevant, children fully understand your work and the issues facing you, especially in relation to maintaining the home/work balance.

4 Build up a range of networks – both inside and outside of work – and you will not only gain by meeting supportive colleagues from different environments, but you will also be able to widen your circle of contacts.

5 Read widely – not just articles and books relating to your immediate area of work, but also informed journals and newspapers which will extend your knowledge of the environment outside your organization and may help you understand the impact of world events on your business.

6 Make sure you keep up to date with relevant training and development courses – they will broaden your skills and knowledge and increase your self-confidence.

7 Become involved in activities outside work – there is mutual benefit in applying what you have learned at work to a leisure interest and in bringing other skills and knowledge to your daily job.

Case study – Theresa

Theresa, 56, is married with three grown-up children and, until recently, was head of Management Learning at the Management College of a UK clearing bank. Following a major reorganization in 1996, her future within the company is not yet certain.

'My ambition when I left school in 1959 was to be a Bohemian, and art school in London was the beginning of my somewhat unconventional adult life. After three years in London, I spent a year in Manchester doing post-graduate work and, to earn extra money, I became involved in social work, running evening classes for boys on probation. The boys taught me a great deal. One boy who had been expelled from every school he had ever been to realized that he could spend time drawing obscene pictures in class and then sell them on. I made him bring them out in the open and make sure they were anatomically correct. He became an engraving apprentice.

'Back in London, finding somewhere to live and a "proper" job led to my first real attempt at networking. I registered with the Design Centre, rang up all my contacts and incredibly found work immediately. A wide range of jobs and experience followed and, included commissions to design murals and dinner services, make silk ties and children's clothes, and being the wardrobe mistress for the Scottish Opera Company, where I learned about difficult people who were too fat for their dresses and about coaching and organization. This busy time in the early 1960s taught me how *not* to run businesses, how to manage people and produce things for money. I learned that if you are honest with people, they trust you more.

'My son, Nicholas, was born in 1966 and I was then faced with the depressing prospect of having to get a "normal" job – whatever that was. I successfully applied for the position of Deputy Display Manager at Lyons, and having been

promoted a while later to Display Manager enjoyed the
relaxed company atmosphere, until it came to a halt when
Lyons sold the Corner Houses. I didn't realize there were
proper company structures, grades and so on – I just used
to go and ask for more money when I wanted it. I was
finally deployed to work in the Film Unit and the Personnel
Manager commented on how much I was earning for a
woman. I had reached the age of thirty without ever really
reporting directly to anyone. Even then I was practically
on my own. I worked out what I thought I ought to be
doing, my boss agreed, shut his door and I got on with
my job. I made myself very useful, took responsibility and
frightened everybody to death!

'I was then offered a job with Eastern Gas which was
conveniently near where we were living, especially as my
husband was beginning to have bouts of illness. (I had met
Geoff when he was working in a different part of the company. I'd been doing some work on casualties and when
Geoff went to the loo he found this man covered in what
looked like blood and promptly administered first aid. I met
him when I went to explain and apologize). At Eastern
Gas, I was sent on all sorts of courses, including one about
producing training packages where I was sent at the last
minute to fill a vacancy. The course itself was not inspiring,
but the effect of being the most junior person there with
fourteen senior (male) colleagues made me realize my own
potential.

Then one day, when I was helping one of the directors
with a presentation about cuts in personnel, I suddenly
realized that I was not going to progress from where I was
and so applied for, and got, a job at TSB designing media
packages. Now, at thirty-nine, I was beginning to understand that I was actually quite ambitious and I was also
aware that I might have to become the family breadwinner.
After a false start with a distance-learning MBA – I didn't
have any spare time and the way they were teaching was

alien to me – I was awarded a Certificate in Business Administration. My work at TSB included launching new products with the Business Development Department, working on computer-based training and, after a move to the new management college in TSB, setting up an audio-visual unit. This was perceived as a great success externally, and I spoke at conferences and won awards, but it was frustrating that I was having to win influence by getting approval from outside the organization and bringing it back inside.

'After a while, I wanted a change of role and took the opportunity to run programmes. This brought in a lot of money. When I was made deputy director of the college, I had already developed strong relationships with policymakers and people and Head Office – understanding the company politics has been *very* helpful. Now, with the merger of Lloyds and TSB, I have moved from Solihull to Bristol and am watching developments within the new organization with great interest.'

EMBRACING CHANGE

'Overall, men receive about the same amount of training as women but some of the reasons why women and men undergo training vary. The most common reason for both women and men is to learn new skills. Men, however, are more likely than women to undergo training because they want to improve their chances of promotion, while women are more likely to want to make their work more interesting.' *Social Focus on Women*, Central Statistical Office, 1995

The nature of learning

The way in which women learn is a topic which many of my interviewees mentioned, particularly as an obstacle to acquiring the necessary skills and knowledge to progress.

As an example, which may strike a chord with many women, Theresa admits that during her first year at art school she didn't understand any of what she was taught – 'but I wasn't the only one – I think it was down to the tutors. What I did learn from this even then was that it was difficult to learn from them, no matter what they *said*, because it was only by *doing* the work with someone coaching me that I was able to learn'. Later, when she enrolled at Warwick University thinking she would like to do a distance-learning MBA in her spare time, Theresa realized that the way they were teaching was alien to her. 'When you go back to school as an adult, you're probably going to learn in a different way. I struggled on and did a year in complete isolation without seeing any of the tutors or students. In the end, I wrote and told them how distance learning *really* works'. Having become aware that interactive materials were a better tool for learning than doing things separately, Theresa went on to produce integrated materials for the courses she designed at a management college.

Carol began her working life as an apprentice and really enjoyed being at work and meeting people. 'I was sent on day release to do a business studies course, but I failed because I wasn't interested. In lectures they just talked at me and I can't take it in when information is presented in that way. I have to have pictures or exercises or projects to complete.' What helped Carol enormously was that during her apprenticeship she visited all the different parts of the business and consequently understood the whole process from start to finish. 'You knew the immediate impact of what you were doing. Later I was able to apply that experience – my common sense helped me to see the whole picture much more clearly than others who had been only theory based.'

The whole approach to education, training and development has changed significantly over the past decade. Before, there existed pockets of innovation – programmes where 'chalk and talk' was not thought to be the best way to teach managers a variety of skills and behaviours – but they were by no means universal. Now, there is a move towards a more widespread use of improved programmed and distance learning, but even here the emphasis is changing towards problem-solving. As each person learns in an individual way, it is important to find the type of course that suits you best and that you will benefit most from.

Finding the right training

There is a wide range of training and development courses available to managers. In recent years there has been a tendency among some training providers to jump on to the equal-opportunities bandwagon by offering courses which are supposed to be designed specifically for women. The danger here is that often these are merely their normal courses with a new name and it is likely that very little has been made to gear them towards the actual needs and aspirations of women. The providers of such programmes need to change their approach dramatically. Instead of dressing up old formats in thinly-disguised new packages labelled 'For Women', they will have to think long and hard about what is *really* required of their tailored courses. Many professional bodies and women's organizations have already requested the views of women members of all ages and backgrounds for help in suggesting the most effective means of achieving worthwhile training schemes.

Attempts to introduce women-only courses may invariably run into opposition. The comparatively small number of senior women does lead to difficulties. A senior manager at a housing association talked about a proposal to run an internal course on breaking through the glass ceiling. It was aimed at women managers, but they knew it would happen only if the male-run administration signed up to the concept. As the men felt it threatened their position, they did not support the idea and it failed. And even if in-house courses are available for women managers, they are not always successful, as shown in the following two examples:

'The problem is that there are not enough women at my level in this organization. Our programmes encourage participation from a wide range of grades – which is good for those women presently in more junior positions, but it often means that the programmes are not challenging enough for the (fewer) senior women.'

'I did attend a senior management course where two inspiring tutors helped us enormously, but the trouble was that all we had in common was being women. While that was fun, it wasn't as developmental as it should have been, because managerially we operated at too diverse levels. I had hoped for so much more. I learnt more by networking with women I found at my own managerial level.'

So what is available in the training and development field?
Training offers to teach new skills, or to build on existing knowledge, with specified results. Effective appraisal systems and discussions with colleagues will highlight gaps in management skills (such as, teamworking, assertiveness and time management), or technical and professional skills (such as aspects of IT, banking, marketing or distribution)

and will therefore help in choosing the appropriate training course.

Courses in management skills are given by both external providers, including specialist training companies and consultants, universities and colleges of further education and professional bodies, and in-company trainers. In some organizations, outside consultants are brought in to run courses, either on their own or with an internal trainer. Many organizations run their own courses and, increasingly, employees are encouraged to devise their own training programmes by choosing the modules most relevant to expanding their particular skills. Where these activities are tailored to the needs of the individual's and the company's needs, and where participants meet colleagues from other parts of the organization, such courses can be extremely helpful.

It is hard to identify the exact developmental skills which are the most beneficial in managers to look at their whole role – rather than at one specific skill – to reflect on their work and the balance of that with home and leisure, and to look to their future. It may therefore be extremely difficult for women managers to find the right activity to address those needs – especially if, as the aforementioned findings of the CSO report suggest, women are less interested in looking for ways to increase their chances of promotion than male managers.

Developmental activities, in their widest context, are based on varied methods of learning and stand in direct contrast to the predominantly lecture/discussion-based training courses. Over the past twenty-five years, I have learned of a great number of programmes of varying quality which addressed the many aspects of personal and professional development. Some courses are for both men and women, others have been designed specifically for women, and I know of one example of how, contrary to usual practice, a women-only programme has been adapted for men (although I'm sure there must be others).

One example of innovative activity stems from the early 1970s, when GEC initiated a senior management development programme using the Action Learning approach. This entailed twenty-one managers from within GEC companies and their client organizations working for eight months tackling tough, real-time projects in different parts of GEC, not only to bring a fresh approach to the issues, but also to learn rapidly and effectively the skills required for senior management. As part of the Action Learning approach, the managers also had to meet regularly in small groups to review, criticize and support each other. A senior, woman civil servant who was seconded to a major manufacturing company reflects on this experience as extremely valuable and, in particular, working with her Action Learning Group.

The Action Learning approach has been developed, honed and modified in many diverse ways over the years. A recent variation was introduced into the NHS under the name of Skill Swap in 1994–95. This initiative was funded by the South Thames Region and offered short-term secondments to employees, so that people with relevant expertise could be brought in to tackle specific problems in another part of the region. The scheme, therefore, provided individuals with an opportunity for personal growth while, at the same time, offering scope for wider organizational development – with staff moving between agencies, sharing expertise and challenging cultural boundaries. Support for the secondees was provided by staff from the Salomons Centre (which is a training and development provider for health and social care attached to Christchurch College, Canterbury), on both a one-to-one basis as mentors and on a group basis in workshops. Secondees were also encouraged to develop their networks as a way of establishing relationships and maintaining contacts which would continue beyond the formal Skill Swap activity. One of the secondees wrote enthusiastically, 'It is one of the most important and exciting developments in the NHS. The whole process is innovative, inspiring, challenging and it has so much to offer every party involved.'

As a direct result of its success the Skill Swap idea is now being considered by several NHS Trusts as part of their personal development strategy, and the NHS Women's Unit has since commissioned the Salomons Centre to design and run a programme specifically aimed to develop women in middle and senior management.

Outdoor activities have received mixed press over the years. In my discussions with women managers, there is an overall perception that men are more likely to try and prove themselves over assault courses and through experiencing physical hardship and danger. The types of activity generally preferred by women are exemplified by a 'Ropes' course which is based on trust and challenge. Here, through an increasingly difficult sequence of activities involving ropes and planks, participants learn how to ask for help from others and, therefore, how to trust them. I know of one senior woman who, at the end of a comparatively simple run of exercises, burst into tears and admitted that in thirty years of work this was the first time she had ever trusted anyone. It was a salutary experience for her and for the people she was working with. One experienced consultant who offers these courses observes that, as a rule, the men try to rush through the early stages of the sequence to reach the more testing activities, while the women generally work their way steadily through everything, building confidence and reinforcing their learning as they progress.

Annual conferences, workshops, seminars and other events staged by professional bodies are seen as useful, particularly from the networking point of view. They may not be specifically geared to women but, where they are, a typical comment is, 'It really helps to talk to other women from different workplaces about the experiences in their own organization'. This is especially important when there are few women at a similar level in one's own organization.

A recent example of a high profile conference was staged by the journal *Management Today* in association with Cranfield School of Management and Cranfield Business Women. 'Women in Management – the New Era' was advertised as being of particular interest to 'women who are looking to develop their potential to the full. Also, those who realize the importance of the feminine style of management and its potentially positive impact on the operation of businesses and organizations will want to attend'. The importance attached to this conference was demonstrated by the quality of its women speakers. Dame Rennie Fritchie (formerly NHS Policy Chair of the South West Regional Health Authority) was in the chair; Glenda Jackson, MP, gave the keynote address and the other speakers included: Dr Susan Vinnicombe, Dean of the Cranfield School of Management; Sheila McKechnie, Director of the Consumers' Association; Liz Forgan, formerly Managing Director, BBC Network Radio; Patricia Vaz, Director, Supply Management, BT Networks and Systems, 1995 Business Woman of the Year; and Professor Anne Huff, Professor of Strategic Management, University of Colorado and Cranfield University.

The traditional MBA programmes and business schools' Executive Programmes act as a general introduction to management science and to the range of business opportunities available. They are particularly useful in introducing participants to a wide range of people and types of organizations, as well as promoting a sense of self-belief. Women members have mentioned how helpful they found the sessions on subjects of which they had little previous experience, for example, finance and the 'numerate dimensions of management'.

Women-only programmes

Women's reactions to women-only courses vary enormously. For many women who have not previously attended any women-only courses they seem like a good idea, as many feel that the atmosphere might be more conducive to honesty and sharing which would provide a welcome antidote to the male-dominated environments in which they work.

Those who have benefited from women-only courses tend to have had similar experiences:

'I always enjoy women-only events because I find that such groups usually reach a high level of openness and trust very quickly and this facilitates useful debate and the opportunity to really concentrate on issues which are usually common to all. I never experience the same level of openness in a mixed group – although being in the minority is the norm for me in the workplace. I have concluded over the years that our outlook tends to be very different from men's and that, too often, there are 'forces' within the organization trying to push me into the male model. These are subtle and effective, but my instincts are that the 'feminine' balance is more important now than ever.'

The networking aspect of women-only programmes is consistently seen as an advantage, especially at a higher level where women work in separate areas of an organization, or with a different industry because of the smaller numbers of women in management generally.

On the other hand, women who could see the pros and cons of both mixed and women-only courses summed up with the following:

'I'm torn, honestly. I want to be treated as an individual, not just as a woman, so in theory I favour mixed courses. However, if a group is not evenly mixed and men predominate, I find it hard to learn. So, if I can't have my first preference of really mixed groups, I favour women-only. (The bonus is that women do genuinely seem more creative).'

'I am ambivalent. On the one hand, I feel that as I do not manage in a women-only environment, then it is not helpful to train in one. However, I recognize that, on the other hand, it may be useful for confidence building and that it can be easier to be open with, and relate to, other women and their experiences.'

'I have never participated in a programme designed specifically for women, although I have run programmes that have been made up of all women and the dynamics of an all-female group has at times created a "cosy" environment where some of the real issues faced can be/have been avoided or denied. I think women-only courses have their place in helping women to explore some of the issues they face. However, the real challenge is in developing effective working relationships with men and learning to utilize their personal power and influence to be equal and yet different in their approach. The challenge is in remaining in touch with our "womenliness" and in not trying to adapt to male role models. Unfortunately, many women who are perceived as "successful" have lost something of themselves in achieving this.'

There are many questions to be asked about women-only courses – one of the main concerns being how they are perceived by others. Often such courses are unfairly labelled as inferior, that is, the women couldn't make it onto the 'real' training schemes which are implicitly run for men. Other concerns raised included the following:

'Although I see the value of them, I have one concern: can they be seen as being discriminatory to men? Courses at senior levels seem to cause a lot of suspicion among the men – is the backlash worth it?'

'Is it a "real" learning situation? There are very few organizations without male managers and so it should be of greater value to learn together.'

This last point was made in one way or another by the majority of women managers.

'Women-only courses have never appealed, because they appear to be about training women to behave more like, or compete with, men.'

'I would prefer to focus on traits which *all* managers have to develop to achieve success for their organization within a framework of equality. Both men and women have to learn these together and deal with any differences they might have as part of the entire learning process.'

'A bad idea. Education and training should focus on individual goals and deficiencies, not on generalized, assumed needs of a particular category of manager. Women are often as different from each other as women are from men.'

'My company used to run women-only courses. The programmes themselves were excellent and provided junior women specialists and managers with several role models at the senior level. However, they do need to take into account a broader development programme for women, rather than stand alone, as they tend to get labelled and often fail to provide the whole range of skills that developing senior managers require to be successful in a male-dominated senior hierarchy.'

Julia made a deliberate choice not to follow a new course, Women in Management, on her MBA programme:

'I felt quite strongly that my career would benefit more from an extra course in management accounting or corporate finance, rather than taking what I saw as a slightly marginal study area. Through other women colleagues, I kept an eye on the content of the course and did not regret my decision.'

When are women-only courses appropriate?

Organizations which run programmes for their female employees – who show management potential – often do so as part of a broader programme, of which the greater part is shared with male colleagues who are also going into management. The women-only training helps to clarify what is possible and how to achieve it. The overwhelming opinion is that it is particularly useful for building confidence and relating to other women and their experiences as well as preparing them for the type of culture in which they will be operating.

Increasingly, women are aware that this type of programme, when available in-house, has to be carefully positioned within organizations and participation should be voluntary with the aims and benefits carefully thought through. Such caution arises from concern about committing disproportionate resources to women, when the real issue is for men and women to learn to work together successfully, and from a desire to lessen the chances of a destructive backlash from men.

There would appear, however, to be two identifiable stages of a woman's managerial career when women-only training programmes may be particularly relevant and where, indeed, they might prove a critical part of development provision for some women:

1 At the beginning of their managerial career, or after a career break, where a programme will build their confidence and accelerate their development.
2 When they have reached a point in their career and life where they may feel they are at a major crossroads. Then, time and space to review what is happening to them now, and what might happen in the future, is a necessary rite of passage.

Research indicates that, for women who have taken a career break, programmes which bring them up to date on the professional and technical developments of their particular field, combined with a 'refresher' on basic management skills, will enable them to face other colleagues at work on a more equal footing. In the late 1980s and early 1990s the trend was for training providers to offer courses for women returners. Over the years these programmes have been refined and developed into more thoughtful and useful activities, giving women a chance to prepare themselves for a very different business environment from the one in which they worked before and, indeed, from the domestic life in which they are going to operate on a less full-time basis.

The second stage, where women often feel that they need some time to reflect, may become apparent once they have progressed successfully to a senior position, when perhaps the family is growing up and leaving home, when the future may seem unclear and, possibly, uninviting. This is a time when the brave make a conscious effort to step back and take stock of the changes and challenges that life has sprung on them.

The Recess College for Senior Executive and Professional Women

I was fortunate to be involved at the setting up of what has proved to be a hugely successful, development activity for senior women; the original concept for which was inspired by Elisabeth Henderson, an experienced consultant. It involves an exciting approach to management development, from which both tutors and participants benefit. Having helped to design the initial programme, and as one of the tutors on the first College in 1988, I was gratified to hear one of the first course attendees describe it as one of the most inspiring and helpful programmes she had ever been on.

'It was multi-dimensional in that it allowed individuals to explore personal and professional issues, and in that it recognized that the historical and cultural positions we came from had left us with development work to do, which could be physical, emotional, mental and spiritual. This was the only programme I had heard of which was willing to try to tackle all the levels.'

Elisabeth Henderson described the original rationale behind the programme thus:

'There were reasons for designing a programme specifically for women. There comes a point at a senior level where women need to look at how they handle issues of achievement, identity, style, motivation and their objectives differently from other colleagues. If women are going to be effective in top management positions, they have to have confidence in their own cultural yardsticks. They need to review their classifications of personal, private, professional, client and employee contexts and to integrate all their learning from home, their understanding of relationships, their management and technical experience in order to feel 'whole', to handle themselves effectively and use their influence in leadership positions.

'What has emerged from the original ten-day programme is remarkable. There is a friendship network, lunches where members from different Colleges get to know one another, review meetings and a vigorous Action Learning activity.'

The College takes place in Oud Poelgeest, a sixteenth-century Dutch castle in Leiden, and the staff includes Dutch and British women who have already experienced the course. This is important as one of the characteristics of the College is the level of commitment to each other's growth and the ability to work seamlessly with each other.

The main reason for the programme's success is not because it is set up as a mini-sabbatical providing managerial skills in the technical sense, but because it goes beyond these parameters to give participants an opportunity to review their work *and* their personal positions, to reflect on achievements – and costs – and integrate their current priorities. At this senior stage of professional and personal life, self-awareness is a precondition of handling change and managing leadership roles.

The women's organizations benefit in turn by the development of their successful women managers and professionals who are able to solve problems in a fresh way, communicate differences in perspective and play a significant role in the leadership of change.

The College is an ongoing scheme for those searching for empowerment in their work, who wish to handle their sphere of influence and develop their personal sense of mission. The core programme is still the ten-day event on leadership, personal and professional renewal, plus follow-up reviews and networking.

In fact, the course has proved so successful that, at the request of male colleagues of the participants, the 'College for Men' has now been firmly established.

The success and merits of any programme depend a great deal on the quality of facilitators and the balance of the programme. It is not easy for people to take out time from work and home. It also takes courage to attend an activity which may make you question many of the tenets by which you have conducted your life so far. It may change your life and that involves taking risks which may impact not only on you but on all those with whom you live and work. Perhaps the people who are prepared to take these kinds of risk if they are to reach the highest levels of achievement at work, are exactly the kinds of people we need to run businesses in the twenty-first century?

ACTION PLAN:

1 Assess your own skills and knowledge from time to time – through appraisal systems, or discussions with your line manager, or colleagues – so that you can make an informed decision about what kind of training you need.

2 Find out – inside or outside your organization – who provides knowledge training and development so that you can choose the course best suited to you.

3 Remember that you need to improve not only your technical and professional knowledge, but also your personal and management skills.

4 Watch out for notice of conferences and other events which may be of interest to you as well as providing a useful networking opportunity.

5 Think carefully about the pros and cons of women-only courses.
6 Look forward to all new experiences as learning opportunities – anticipate excellence from others – you may be pleasantly surprised.

CRITERIA FOR SUCCESS

'I would consider myself both successful and fulfilled within my job which is very satisfying. Real accomplishment is a mixture of external recognition of a job well done and an internal belief that you've been able to create meaning and a set of beliefs and values to that job which enriches one's own working life. To have all aspects of oneself represented through one's work is indeed a joy. That things are not merely accomplished, but at the same time create a sense of self-esteem, fun and purposefulness for oneself and those working with you is very positive. An opportunity to grow and learn and operate in a challenging and supportive environment is essential.'
  Margaret Elward

How do we measure success

What do we mean by 'success' and how do we quantify it? In women managers' answers to that question, there are differences in detail, but otherwise a great deal of consistency.

There is no doubt that being employed in a high-level job, with its accompanying status, is tremendously important to many women. As is the satisfaction of being selected for promotion or, as one woman was pleased to say, 'My last three jobs have been found for me'. To have been able to affect people's and organizations' lives in a positive way –

'to be in a high-influencing sphere' – is of considerable value to women: 'I know I have always managed to leave organizations, people and places in better shape than when I joined.'

Being well-regarded in your field and building a reputation for your ability to achieve results is seen as a measure of success. 'On an individual basis, I can perform well to targets'; or, 'My measurement of success has always been in terms of service to clients, and to deliver our programmes to cost and on time. To achieve this requires energy and an immense amount of management skill to motivate staff to react and respond to deadlines.'

Knowing that other people's perception of you is of a successful manager is also a source of gratification, and positive feedback from family, friends, colleagues, staff and customers is always welcome. To have broken into the top echelons of a traditionally male-dominated organization is, indeed, cause for celebration – 'For a long time, I was the only female partner in a worldwide partnership of ninety, but others are slowly emerging'. When this also involves becoming a role model for others, women finally begin to believe in their success – although sometimes there seems to be an element of: 'It was hard to realize they were talking about me. It still surprises me that I am perceived as successful.' We all recognize the warm glow you feel when you know that you've progressed further in your career than you expected, that you've surpassed even your own expectations.

Another, equally important, measure of success for women involves their relationships with others who work with them. It is vital that their staff are highly motivated and involved. A typical comment is: 'My staff provide feedback that I manage in a way which empowers them and makes them feel supported and able to develop', a view reinforced by: 'I now have a team which is recognized as functioning well in my absence'. The encouragement of colleagues so that they work hard and produce good results, are happy, fulfilled and loyal, is of major concern to most women managers.

There seems to be a need to be part of a two-way relationship between themselves and their staff, colleagues, customers and even the environment in which they operate. Women managers feel most comfortable in an atmosphere where they can learn and adapt – 'I strive to obtain honest and constructive comments from those I trust to help my learning'.

To this, they add good customer feedback, a productive, friendly working relationship with their peers and the achievement of strategic goals.

The issue of maintaining a workable and acceptable balance between professional and personal lives is one by which women managers judge their success. The achievement of this goal ranks as one of the most sought after and probably the most difficult to attain. 'I am efficient in my time management and cope well with stress and pressure' was one woman's reaction, but a more typical response was: 'I have a reasonable balance between home and work, although I sometimes find that my personal life is more limited'. One woman who knows that she achieves the required work performance in a style which carries people with her and allows them to develop, thinks that she will really be able to call herself successful when, 'I have time to ensure that my staff can give their best to the company whilst having compatible personal objectives.'

High financial reward is not usually top of the list as prime evidence of success, although most managers value the extra flexibility that a good income offers in balancing the component parts of their lives. One woman who considers herself successful – because she knows she is good as her job and that her staff are committed to her – feels simultaneously that she is not as successful as she would like to be 'because I am denied the money and status of my male colleagues – but to challenge this would risk too much'.

The present generation of younger women managers are prepared to challenge this issue of equal pay. They know that to ignore it is to perpetuate the inequality and they expect to receive the same remuneration for the same work.

Most women who have reached managerial positions do acknowledge their success and are more than happy to point out the areas where they feel they contribute to their organizations, but they are also realistic enough to admit to limitations: 'My job is about managing clients and a peer group, rather than directing a large number of subordinates which is not a skill set I believe I have, or would ever have.'

The confidence gained with reaching a high position and knowing that you are capable of the work involved is sometimes a little fragile: 'I lack the confidence and "toughness" to be an effective manager of people. I find individuals under my "span of control" exceedingly difficult to handle'. Even when women feel they are successful in their own terms, they sometimes wonder how they can reconcile their opinion with other people's perceptions of them: 'I'm mostly successful in terms of my own personal values, but not in terms of the values of some of the male managers I've worked with', and: 'If "successful" means when all those to whom I am accountable think I am successful, then with my clients, the answer is "yes", with my staff, "usually", but with my board, "no".'

Many women managers are extremely self-critical: 'I always feel that I could do better. I strive to be a good manager, but I don't think that I've got it quite right yet!' However, during recent years, women are beginning to acknowledge their own skills and talents and the importance of their contribution to management within their organizations. They worry a lot about getting it right, but are getting better at saying they are good at what they do, whether it is dealing with the 'people' side or achieving goals and targets. They depend a great deal on the feedback from others, but the emphasis is changing from: 'I need to know that people like me' to 'I need to know that what I'm doing is appropriate for the people and the organization, so that I can learn and adapt'.

Women managers are adjusting the yardsticks of success by the introduction of their unique skills and values and are, therefore, redefining the rules by which companies are run. While accepting the need to meet financial targets and other 'hard' evidence of profitability and achievements of goals, women are also stressing the importance of 'soft' aspects by, for example, introducing ways of measuring employees' behaviours and attitudes into performance appraisal systems.

'I would measure success by the nature of one's accomplishments: reputation, effective working relationships with subordinates, colleagues and superiors; and by one's ability to sustain a career over time with a satisfying personal life. I am not equating success with happiness in life, but it should be more enduring than meeting this quarter's earning projections. I would recognize success in myself more easily if I had ten times my current net worth, or some other badge of wild material success, but this is a measure created by the media in our culture (it would nonetheless be nice if it weren't for the trade-offs!). I also think one should always have something to aim for – so success is continually reappraising one's goals. In this sense, success is not an end point and may always be out of reach.'

ACTION PLAN:

1 Think about what being successful means to you – a feeling of self-worth, material possessions, high financial reward, status, respect from your work colleagues, satisfying personal relationships, and so on. This will help you choose the type of environment you wish to work in.

2 Consider how your organization, colleagues, friends and family perceive success – how does this tie in with your criteria?

3 Be critical of yourself, but be realistic in your demands and acknowledge your own skills and talents.

4 Re-assess your criteria for success from time to time as your circumstances change.

5 Reward yourself when you have achieved important goals.

Case study – Zoë

Zoë, 46, is married with two children. She has a degree in Biological Sciences and Social Studies and is one of three Assistant Directors in a local council in London.

'I'm very adaptable, which I think stems from going to various schools before finishing up at a College of Further Education to sit my O and A levels. I wanted to be a doctor, but someone said it was too tough – physically and intellectually – for a girl, so I chose pharmacology instead. I was accepted at Chelsea College, but soon realized the whole thing was a mistake. There were plenty of women's politics going on and I was studying extra course units in subjects like women and psychology, and science and society. I was lucky to have my year out in a "proper job" with the Clinical Research Centre, at Northwick Park Hospital, researching into nutrition. When I returned to complete my final year I knew I didn't want to be a pharmacologist, but Chelsea didn't like failures so they helped me obtain a degree in Biological Sciences and Social Studies. I went on to begin a PGCE – but realized that too was a mistake. I was still an idealist and believed that *all* people were bright and had potential. I ended up having a huge row with one of the lecturers because he didn't agree, and I walked out never to return.

'There I was, unemployed and without the teaching certificate, so I registered with the Professional and Executive Register and ended up working for an insurance brokers. It wasn't a proper job, so I passed myself off as a secretary and worked briefly for International Voluntary Service. In 1975, flicking through *New Society*, I noticed an advertisement for Committee Co-ordinators at Hammersmith and Fulham Council and was chosen with five others from 160 applications. I was lucky to be placed in a department that was forward looking and which believed in developing people, not in a formal way, but by not saying "No" if you wanted to do something. My first boss was a real mentor for me.

At this time, I became heavily involved in the trades unions. I applied for and gained various promotions as they arose, and I never felt there were any barriers because I was a woman. The only instance of this occurred when I applied for the post of Head of the Programme Unit which was a brand new function, and I didn't get it. They offered it to a man who turned it down and then asked me to do it – but for less money. In all, I was there for about nine years involved in all sorts of amazing things, which you can't do in local authorities now because they're so decentralized.

'I've had a lot of opportunities in my career and have experienced high levels of stress. For a while I worked as lead officer to help create the Women's Department and for nine months was covering two jobs. I applied for and won the position of Assistant Director of Central Services, in Hammersmith, (again in two bites – when no one was chosen the first time, I was offered it the second time). That was my first major management job and I moved to Camden having begun to feel unhappy about the way things were going in Hammersmith and Fulham. Until last year I was Assistant Director, Strategy and Support, when I moved to another local authority and chose my own job title of Corporate Director, Partnership and Responsibility.

'A vital component of my success is that my husband and I are a complete partnership, totally balanced. I have tried to behave in a similar way both at work and home rather than acting out a role as a manager, aping the boys, and I feel increasingly more comfortable with that now. I've been trying to be truer to myself at work – to say what I think, rather than what will get me promoted, and to behave in ways which *I* think are appropriate. It's been very tough making the transition.

'At work I still have the positive conviction that I can develop myself further and I'm doing things that are challenging, because one day I intend to be a chief executive.'

KEEPING THE BALANCE

Women are working hard towards achieving and maintaining a balance between the major parts of their lives and are conscious that often they take on the onus for realizing this rather than their partners.

They may also have to convince others that they are capable of this. It is unusual at interviews for prospective employers to ask men how they will achieve the balance between work and home life, although it is a common question for women.

The prevailing problem for interviewers seems to be how women will cope with young children while they are at work. Theresa tackled this problem early on in her career – when a potential boss asked how she would manage with her baby when he rang up at the weekends, asking her to do some extra work. 'I told him I wouldn't work in the evenings, or at weekends, and wouldn't give him my phone number and he said, "Quite right, you can have the job".'

However, the issue goes wider than just children, and Theresa has also had to face some difficult decisions more recently:

> 'I have taken a hard line with my husband, Geoff's, illness. If the doctors think he's all right to be at home, then he is all right to be at home on his own and, when he's not, I can take time off. I don't know how I would cope only looking after Geoff, because perhaps it is all the other things that keep me going.'

A number of highly-successful women are aware that they are inclined to over-compensate in terms of work levels so that no one can question their professionalism or commitment, or point a finger at them even though they've been told that they no longer have to prove themselves.

It is not easy to make the decision to continue working when the children are still young. Beverley says, 'I felt very reluctant to "abandon" my children (then three- and six-years-old). However, my son put it all into perspective. When I returned home from my first full day, he rushed up to me saying, "How much have you earned today?" By the second day, the family had accepted the normality of mum working full time – to the extent that they didn't even turn round from "Neighbours".'

A vital element of success for women with partners is that they operate as a partnership, completely balanced. Many more of today's generation of women are choosing not to have children and they are not bothered by their decision. A few years ago, if you were successful and did not have children, some people, or sectors of society, felt you weren't complete. For many others, having children is extremely important and not a route to be avoided. They know that they will have to struggle to get the balance right so that they have sufficient time at home and that includes being firm but fair about how much they devote to their work.

Alison and her husband took a deliberate decision not to have children, 'because I don't believe that women can have it all or, at least, not without affecting their relationships with their children and their husband, leaving no time for themselves'.

It is unlikely that women who work are all able to strike the right balance immediately. At the various stages in your working life, demands change and Sarah recognizes that when she says, 'I am thoroughly enjoying myself, but I am obsessed so the balance is not there at the moment. It will come, but I need to focus on the business now. I am driven, but I know it will do very well'.

ACTION PLAN:

1 Be reasonable in your demands on yourself and your relationship with both home and work.
2 Be firm, but fair, with your work colleagues about how much time you devote to your job.
3 Inform your family and friends about your work to the extent that they understand when your job makes extra demands on you from time to time.
4 Talk to friends and colleagues who are combining home and family with work and find out what they do to achieve a balance (or what they discovered was not successful).
5 Don't feel pressured to get married, have children or live a conventional lifestyle if that is not what you want. On

the other hand, don't apologize if that is what you do want.

6 Take time to re-assess your priorities as your circumstances change.

7 Learn techniques to handle pressure – perhaps you could learn yoga or some form of meditation; develop outside interests; make sure you eat sensibly and have enough sleep; allow time for yourself; and, when you talk to yourself, be encouraging and supportive, not over-critical.

Case study – Melanie

Melanie 26, is married with no children and works as a Service Delivery Manager with a large IT consultancy. She left school at sixteen and joined the Bank of England with a view to becoming an international banker, but ended up in the computer centre. When the Bank outsourced several of its computer staff, Melanie joined the consultancy and has since progressed rapidly. In particular she enjoys the people management side of her job and gains a great deal from the management training courses her company provides.

'I went to a comprehensive where the sixth form had 1000 pupils. My weakest subject was English – although I always enjoyed reading – and my strongest Maths, but by the time I left it was the other way round. Partly because of the teachers and partly because of the way the course was set out, I found Maths dull. I had planned to go on to sixth form, but my results weren't so good and having come back from a brilliant holiday I didn't want to go back to school. My mother said that I could only leave school if I had a good job to go to, so I applied to the Bank of England, Barclays and NatWest for interviews. I was offered jobs at all three, even though I arrived two hours late for the NatWest appointment. In the end, I chose the Bank of England because of its kudos. It was the lowest paid of the three by far, but the holidays were so good I went for it.

'I had never touched a computer before and wanted to get into the international banking side, so they put me into the computer centre to learn some skills. I started as admin/receptionist before moving on to the help desk as an operator on mainframes and pcs. I enjoyed it, though looking back it was a doss – plenty of time to do everything. In July 1992 we were taken over by Cap Gemini, because the Bank outsourced forty-one members of the computer staff, and I moved with them.

'From then on my career took off. Prior to that I hadn't even thought about a career. I stayed in the mainframe environment for a year before becoming restless. I went for an interview with a construction company and got the job, but on the same day Cap Gemini offered me work on the desktop side. From then my job took off further. I moved to help-desk analyst – right place at the right time, and hard work, too. One of the team leaders moved to another account and her replacement wasn't due for a few weeks and they needed someone in the meantime to keep it ticking over. My manager said that although I was on a low level they would give me the chance. Luckily, I didn't mess up and even made a few good suggestions. If you were prepared to put the effort in, Cap Gemini would give you the chance. They don't discriminate at all.

'Another opportunity came along, leading a team of about nine people, and it grew from there up to seventeen employees. It could have seemed daunting to find yourself managing people who are graduates above you, but my strength is people management so I have found that quite easy. Yet another opportunity came up, this time within the CSC (Customer Service Centre). My boss had moved on and she recommended that I take over. I thought, "easy" – was I naive. For the first eight to twelve weeks I drowned under the workload and so went to talk to my new boss and said that I thought I couldn't cope. He said, "You can do it, we can have daily meetings, I will point you in the right directions and we will see how it goes". Then I woke up one day and it all clicked. I had been in this environment for four years and I told the company I really need to move on. Service Delivery Management seemed to me the next stage. We have a Service Delivery Programme and I am on that. I have a mentor who I speak to regularly.

'It seems that I have moved on very quickly. I was head-hunted last year – rather flattering – but the woman was condescending because I was so young and hadn't been to university. You don't need a degree to do what I do. If I had stayed on at school and gone on to university, I probably wouldn't have got a job because of the recession. I have been lucky, but I have worked hard. You have to reach for opportunities with both hands. The future is a bit hazy at the moment. I have set myself targets, but I don't expect to achieve them straightaway. My career has caught me a bit unawares. I would be happy to do this job up to a maximum of three years but feel that it's important to keep with the people management side.

'I am married. My husband has his own business and he is proud of what I have achieved. If we have children I would want to take a career break and work from home. Have the children quickly and take five years out. I would want to continue working – I need the buzz I get out of it.

'My mother would have loved it if I had gone to university because she didn't go, but neither of my parents forced the issue. I have two older half-brothers – one is a Eurobond dealer and the other's in marketing.

'The only downside is that I don't seem to have much spare time recently: I used to love skiing, and enjoyed going away on holiday. I used to play sport, but haven't done so for a while – although I'd like to take up in-line skating or roller blading, again.

'I have not found Cap Gemini to be prejudiced – it recognizes that without its staff it will not grow or succeed, so it make the effort with training and encouraging people. I have deliberately steered myself towards the managerial type of training, developing leadership skills, team management workshops – all geared to improving work performance.'

PART TWO
Managing for the Millennium

THE 21ST CENTURY MANAGER – THE SHAPE OF THINGS TO COME

According to the Institute of Management's report, *Management Development to the Millennium*, the skills that managers in the next century will have to possess include: strategic planning, responding to and managing change, total quality management, verbal communication, coaching others and delegating responsibility.

I wondered whether the women managers I had spoken to would have any comments to make about this list, with particular reference to the contribution they had each made to the practice of management for the next century. Although there was some initial hesitation about stereotyping people or making generalizations, there was a mutual agreement that women do seem to have an innate ability in many of the skills mentioned. However, in tune with other comments about the need for men and women to learn to work together, their main concern was that everyone will need to acquire these skills to be successful managers.

'We need a mixture of stereotypical traits to achieve a high standard of management in organizations, particularly at the senior level.'

Many women managers mention the parallel between management and parenting or home-making skills (especially in households where women are the primary homemakers *and* go out to work). Although one manager added, '. . . but, of course, these are skills learned through traditional women's work and are therefore devalued'.

Women are flexible. Traditionally they have spent their lives fitting in with others and responding to their demands. Maintaining the balance between home and work means that responding to change and adapting becomes instinctive, as does the ability 'to operate simultaneously at a variety of levels, putting yourself in other people's shoes; for example, as a customer – again, a life skill for most women'. Indeed, several of the managers interviewed felt that women would not just be responding to change, but that they would be leading cultural change in their organizations.

At this time of turbulent and often threatening change, managers need to discover ways of dealing with disruptions and upheavals, whilst maintaining a degree of stability for those around them. The views of one woman manager on how her female colleagues might handle such uncertainty are interesting: 'I see managers as existing only because of change. If the world were static, everyone would know what to do, so they wouldn't need managing. Management is about creating the environment in which others can thrive and perform well. Indeed, managing change is the skill both of the present and of the future. And, yes, looking about me, I see more women than men who are able to respond in a non-threatening way to the "soft" skills that a climate of change requires. Some men can, too, but there does seem to be a gender advantage for women. Nurture or nature, I can't say . . .'

This viewpoint was further underlined by another comment: 'Future managers will constantly need to initiate change and at the same time help people to see it as an adventure rather than as a threat'.

An experienced senior manager in local authority said: 'The key skills in strategic planning and responding to change involve the ability to plan and take action on several issues at once, while being organized enough to inspire staff that you know where you're taking them and that there's no need to panic.' She then encapsulated what many women see as one of their major assets. 'Multi-priority juggling is something I think more women are better at than men'.

As a slight digression, I was also interested to discover exactly what women managers thought about the importance of strategic planning for organizations in the twenty-first century. The role of strategic planning in business has perhaps been ambiguous and, consequently, misunderstood over the years. The word 'planning' here is a misnomer if it refers to the process whereby senior managers and directors look to the future by taking an overview of the organization and its environment – drawing up scenarios of possible futures and setting strategy which will determine policy. This process should more correctly be called strategic thinking and I have been intrigued to find that most of the women I have spoken to, whilst talking about strategic planning, have quite naturally used the word 'thinking'. That may be because they are more interested in being sensitive to future possibilities rather than getting into the essential, but mechanical, processes of planning'.

For example, 'In my experience, women are well able to understand the concept of strategic planning. It's no accident that the majority of policy managers in my organization are women – many of whom, like me, work for male bosses who lack the breadth of vision needed to plan for the future', and 'Many women can be more holistic in their thinking, I've noticed'.

It is generally accepted that the broad scope of interpersonal skills is seen as an area in which women tend to be more accomplished than men, and consequently more suited to the demands of the changing business environment leading into the twentieth-first century. Women talk a lot about being more perceptive to the feelings of others and of being able to express their feelings more easily than their male counterparts. They are seen to be 'very much aware of the group and caring for the whole'. One manager talked of women as: 'not having egos to protect and seeming to be more trusting, generally, of each other'.

If women are more relationship oriented than men, it follows that a list of skills which includes coaching and communication will closely fit their management style. Mothers have a natural role as coaches to their children: 'You have to be able to constantly readjust the amount of "freedom" to give a child when it tries to do something and usually mothers develop this skill more than fathers'. This is, of course, tied in with delegating skills – in which the abilities to make yourself understood and to encourage others to do something, which you are probably dying to do yourself, are compensated for by the 'sheer joy of helping someone else achieve potential'.

The coaching theme constantly recurred throughout the discussions and interviews undertaken for this book. Among Sarah's aims is that of 'establishing a training scheme that teaches youngsters the things that are important – quality, service and a desire to do the job well'.

It is important to emphasize the key skills of working closely with others and supporting them. 'Every manager should realize that it is their responsibility to support the people who work for them. When I came to this company, that concept didn't exist. The notion that your manager was there for you was completely unknown. I've always been given to work for me the people who were seen to be troublemakers, those who had problems. Mostly they were just frustrated but, with the right kind of inspiration, they usually turned out to be absolute crackers. It was wonderful to watch them blossom and grow. That is the best thing about working with people – you just give them the key and encourage them to find their own way. Recognizing that people have potential – that's what I like.'

When managers have a wide range of tasks for which they are accountable, delegation becomes a necessity if the job is to be accomplished. A common theme was expressed by one manager as: 'It is also a natural way of doing things if you believe in letting people "grow" – so delegation and coaching go hand in hand'. A woman manager in a local authority said of delegating, 'I do believe that men are more conscious of *Power*, whereas women are perhaps more interested in *Influence*; so a much larger number of men are scared of releasing things down to their subordinates, or of developing them'. Following on this theme, another woman stated, 'Lots of men derive their power from withholding information, whereas women want to involve others and therefore tend to communicate well'.

While few women disagreed with the list of skills set down in the Institute of Management's report, most of them felt it was rather limited and had their own ideas on how to expand it to suit the reality of working for companies and organizations in the next century. For example, one of the women said: 'I think imagination and courage will become more important, as will social responsibility and sense of purpose for companies', while another pointed out: 'But organizations will need expertise in financial control to underpin all these other skills'. Indeed, several women made a point of including the harder financial and analytical skills as well.

The ability to balance personal and professional lives is also seen as a crucial requirement for successful women managers. They need to learn to 'align their personal and professional selves to ensure that they can function as a whole person and can fulfil their potential. They must allow themselves to develop along these lines, so they do not have to adopt a "work" persona and a "domestic" persona in potential conflict'. Maintaining this balance and coping with stress are vitally important, as the problem of balancing home and work life has the potential to restrict the career development of a great many women.

Sheila Forbes, who was until recently Director of Human Resources at Reed Elsevier plc, identifies yet another set of skills as becoming progressively important: 'This is to do with multi-cultural management. Increasing numbers of companies are doing business internationally, competition is no longer national – even for some medium/small companies – and acquiring the skills of managing successfully in different cultures will become more and more essential. This adds a further dimension to the already complex career-management issues for women, because it means developing language skills and accepting secondments outside the home country'.

Working together, or 'consensual management', and the ability to pool the appropriate skills, knowledge and experience from a variety of sources are also going to be important. In the words of one manager, 'I believe a more important area of expertise will be harnessing effort/energies from different parts of the organization and often from disparate organizations – through joint working, joint ventures and consortia – possibly using direct lines of authority'.

Overall, there was a significant expression of optimism for the future and for the role that women will play in the management of organizations. In some businesses, it is already happening: 'During my time with my previous company, the requirements for the "new manager" as part of our culture change programme *automatically* qualified more women for these roles. Women were seen to be better coaches and communicators, and sometimes willing to take more risks'.

Many women managers feel that both organizations and society as a whole are changing as we approach the twenty-first century. 'The caricature of the autocratic male boss versus the caring, sharing female boss is a little out of date. I am genuinely optimistic about the next generation, where these skills and styles are given more emphasis amongst both sexes.'

Most women managers were keen to stress that any such list of skills should not be seen to apply to *either* men *or* women, but to *both* men *and* women – but that, at the same time, women need to be conscious of the positive part they have to play in successful companies of the future.

> 'All the skills above are important to all managers and therefore any manager – male or female – deficient in them would be challenged. I believe that women do need to establish and *assert* their way of doing things by demonstrating success on their own terms within a male/aggressive institutional culture'.

There is a strong awareness of the need for men and women to learn and develop these management skills together, for them to continuously learn about themselves and each other and each individual's particular style. Indeed, in spite of many years of opposition from men at work and at home, women managers are keen to redress the balance without acrimony and to work with their male colleagues. 'Many men need assistance in helping to align their domestic and professional lives because, traditionally, male self-esteem needs have been largely pursued in their working lives. They need assistance in developing their inner side – that is, their personal needs within the world of work and through the expectations placed upon them.'

Sheila Forbes summarizes the situation from her experience at the top of an international organization thus:

> 'Although management literature is full of good advice about empowerment and more developmental styles of management, the pressures for high performance

within an internationally competitive business world mean that successful managers will still have to achieve high standards, manage costs tightly, constantly look for improvements in productivity and manage people in a low inflation environment. Those pressures aren't going to go away, and women have to meet those requirements, too. The question is, can they do it in a different way? A better way? Can we be tough on performance, yet still make people feel good about themselves, their work and their contribution?'

In articles and discussions about the specific skills women bring to management, self-organization, people management and attention to detail are all mentioned as key points. Above all, though, it is women's ability to manage their time – often because they have brought up children and run households, as well as holding down a paid job. Women are seen as being less likely to waste time than their male colleagues. The traditional male tendency of staying in the office whether they are needed or not, has not been taken up by women who have to get away to deal with the other aspects of their lives. They don't waste so much time in meetings, recognizing that a great deal of time is lost in long irrelevant discussions, and on the whole women don't call meetings just before it's time to go home.

Case study – Sarah
Sarah, 40, is Managing Director of her own business, Bourneriver Marketing Communications Limited.

'I come from a privileged family background, where money and social opportunities played their part. But my father went bankrupt when I was still young and I had to rely on my own resourcefulness and entrepreneurial skills to survive. I strongly believe in the value of education and, against the odds, did well at school and, at the end of the 1970s, I went to Oxford Poly. No one who gave me career advice ever mentioned PR. I just wish someone had suggested being a magazine editor – I would have loved that. The careers officer suggested I try teaching, which my father agreed with, so out of sheer cussedness I decided against it. So, having completed my degree, I did a secretarial course and went to work as a graduate trainee at Readers Digest, where I learned, for the first time, invaluable promotional skills.

'Having married, I moved with my husband to the Midlands and found a job with Marks & Spencer on a community programme they were running. The work I did there, learning from an experienced manager who didn't have any hang-ups about women, became a model for other enterprise agencies.

'I feel that I have been very fortunate because, although my elder sisters had benefited from the family wealth when they were young, I was beginning my career just when PCs were coming to the fore and I was fascinated in the product. My marriage ended – it had never really got off the ground – and I moved back south, finding work with some of the PR agencies. I learned what I could from them, but having my own ambitions I noticed where the company failed and succeeded and then started my own business. This had a rocky and expensive start as my partner – personal and business – turned out to be real trouble. Eventually I bought the name off him, gave him everything, and inherited a huge pile of debts. In 1993, I re-registered the company and let my clients know that I was still in business. They probably didn't know just how hard it was to keep things going.

'I now have a well-established "bread-and-butter" business, known for being professional, persistent and for providing quality and service. In a recent Spikes Cavell survey, we were cited as being one of three PR firms which topped the strategic relationships league table, and as one of the four best overall PR performers from a client perspective.

'I am self-taught, yet I've learned a lot working with the journalists who are always talking with the captains of industry. I've always said I wanted to be a millionaire, mainly to restore the family fortune to my mother. I want to prove to myself that I can do it. I could not have lived with myself if I had given up. I now know what I can achieve – I'm building for the future. I want Bourneriver to stand for quality.'

LOOKING FORWARD

'Women's perceptions of themselves and of their place in society have changed dramatically over the last twenty-five years owing to social factors and to the immense influence of feminist thought and action and I recognize the values of organizations shifting to reflect social changes, albeit slowly. The real problem now is that men have not caught up, have not educated themselves, or been trained adequately to deal with this social revolution.'

How could training and development for women managers be improved?

While women managers in some sectors may feel that much is being done in the field of equal opportunities on a general scale – for example, those working in the NHS or local government – there are still three main areas of training and development which were consistently mentioned as needing greater attention, with a strong case for addressing specific needs and acquiring particular skills coming within those three groups:

1 Professional Support Systems:
  career advice
  counselling
  networking
  mentors
2 Personal Support Systems:
  maintaining balance
  integrity
  flexibility
3 Interpersonal Support Systems:
  working with men
  informing and educating men
  valuing differences

*Professional Support Systems: career advice/counselling/
networking/mentors*

A recurring theme is that women need to be more proactive
in designing their own worklives: 'Women need to become
better at managing their careers and *owning* their career
management in ways that their male counterparts are
brought up to do. I still hear few women setting themselves
goals and ambitions with respect to work, in the habitual
manner that ambitious, high-potential young men talk and
present themselves'.

Women recognize that one of the major obstacles is their
own expectation of what the future holds for them,
whether this stems from the home or school environment
in which they have been brought up, or from their first
experiences of the world of work. Beginning the process of
planning and thinking through the available options during
their latter years at school would be a positive first step for
most women. It should then be easier to continue this process at the various transitional stages of their lives, negotiating with increasing skill and confidence for what they want,
in setting goals, in influencing others and in developing
their own style. 'Women still need help in thinking through

their options and in finding the courage to negotiate for what they want. Not enough of this type of advice is available using frameworks which are meaningful for women.'

A natural consequence of encouraging women to establish regular, personal reviews would be the establishment of professional networks and access to mentors who would play their advisory role in supporting and developing another woman's career. It is necessary for all managers to continuously update their individual levels of professional knowledge, skill and competence in their jobs, and personal development plans (PDPs) now feature regularly in many organizations' performance appraisal schemes. In fact, the Ashridge Management Index (1996) particularly stresses the importance and growing popularity of PDPs for all managers.

The Ashridge Index also mentions that, as a result from their research among participants on their courses, men and women are equally likely to be offered almost all of the management development initiatives available within organizations, 'except for one – mentoring'. The report goes on to say that 'this difference between men and women is an important issue of which organizations should take note. Earlier work by Ashridge, examining the career development process in the information technology sector, found that mentoring was 'a key factor in helping to ensure women were on an equal footing with their male colleagues'.

Mentoring and coaching as a form of support for managers has become increasingly popular over the last few years, and some specialist consultancies provide a much-appreciated service to managers and directors. It has become progressively common for organizations to offer executives access to mentors or, in the case of senior executives, to external coaches as part of their career development. In such cases, they are given a list of people who would make suitable mentors and also a budget to cover the cost of spending time with their preferred choice. An important part of this system is that it is understood that any conversations between the manager and mentor are strictly confidential and that the manager's company will not approach the coach for information or progress reports on its employee.

Encouraging women to develop and gain from support networks is seen as an important skill to foster, together with an innate understanding of what networking can do for a career path. One example is the growth of women's industry groups, which many managers have found helpful. (Several contact address are given at the end of the book.)

Personal Support Systems: maintaining balance/integrity/ flexibility

One commonly expressed emotion is guilt, which often runs parallel to the recognition that women need to free themselves from this feeling: 'My biggest obstacle is overcoming the guilty feeling of not being able to be perfect at everything, i.e., mother, wife *and* employee'. As one woman pointed out, 'We would benefit from counselling on how best to deal with the domestic versus work choices which we all have to make. This isn't just needed for women managers though'.

The suggestion that women will not fully develop their career potential and learn to channel their energies into *themselves*, as well as into others, and to be true to themselves was echoed in a variety of ways. Women gain more satisfaction in their dealings with both work and home once they stop trying to be different people in the two roles. Instead of merely accepting that the present unsatisfactory situation exists, and adjusting their needs and aspirations within that framework, women are now beginning to bend the 'rules' to suit their lifestyles: that is, they are questioning the traditional way that things have been done and are striving for alternative approaches to managing resources.

Childcare provision (or the care of any dependants) falls within this category. The choices are expanding for both the employer and the employee. Some organizations, while not offering either financial or practical aid, do enable employees to juggle their dual existence at their own discretion. Other companies may offer a contribution towards childcare; others may provide a nursery with subsidized places and there are some employers who offer an annual lump sum to be put towards a child's nursery place, a car, a season ticket, and so forth.

Susan Hay, who runs her own consultancy as well as a string of workplace nurseries, gave an example of how attitudes to retaining good female staff on the workforce have evolved over the past five or six years. Recently, at one of her nurseries, a parent had mentioned that her employer and colleagues were upset because she wasn't at her computer by 8.00 in the morning. She arrives at work at 8.05 a.m., because the nursery opens at 8.00 a.m. She wanted the nursery to open at 7.45 a.m., but their research indicated that there wouldn't be a big enough demand to justify the cost, so they said they couldn't do that. She went back to her boss and told him the outcome. His response was, 'That's OK. I know how hard you work and how happy you are with those childcare arrangements – which means you work well and productively while you're here'. Susan feels that six years ago the response to this woman would have been very different. 'Today I think people can expect some negotiation – some room for manoeuvre – because we now understand that proper childcare is essential to the wellbeing of employees. It is not simply a question of throwing money at a problem and not wanting to hear any more about it. It is relevant to productivity at work that there is a different climate now, and it's a much healthier attitude than going down the benefits route.'

As long as structural barriers remain, such as the length of time spent at work each day, women managers will welcome the increase in open-learning facilities which make it easier to fit studies around domestic commitments. The increase in opportunities for job swaps, secondments and so on, is also a step in the right direction, although there is still a great deal to be done in this area.

Women need to be able to develop their own style as managers, to be effective in their work and appropriate in their actions. It's vital that women feel they have permission to demonstrate their natural flexibility by ensuring that they have access to the full range of behaviours available, whilst recognizing that they may use them in a different way from their male colleagues. This includes 'the strong, assertive or directive behaviours some people do not associate with women, or that women are scared of using (or were told not to at an early age)'. This issue leads on to the third area – where much work has yet to be done – that is, how men and women work together.

Interpersonal Support Systems: working with men/ informing and educating men/valuing differences
The most striking correlation of all the conversations I have had with women managers is their desire to create an environment in which men and women can learn to work together. Because women understand the reality of having to operate in a world in which the two sexes work together, they accept that it is unrealistic to concentrate on either men's or women's development at the expense of the whole. They recognize that there exists as broad a range of management styles within the female population as there is within the male population, and that this should perhaps be the starting point rather than assumptions based on sex. The majority of women believe that through informing and educating men and by valuing the different working styles, men and women can successfully work together in a posi- tive and fulfilling environment.

How, then, can this change in attitude be accelerated? In

some of the more traditional organizations, the acceptance
of women as equal members of the workforce at all levels
is taking time to gain true credence. In others, particularly
in certain sectors of public service, the stereotypes are being
eroded more easily because a greater degree of time and
effort is being allocated to training and development.
Women managers in such sectors are therefore gaining a
considerable amount of experience which could be passed
on to others charged with looking at equal opportunities
within their organizations and they are in an ideal position
to take some responsibility for publicizing the reality of
what is actually possible:

> 'I believe more training and development should be
> available to those "with power" about the issues facing
> women with regard to their development. This is best
> dealt with when women are already successful and are
> able to raise issues as equals with their male peers.'

As already mentioned in the section on what is available
in the area of training and development, one of the most
helpful courses for both aspiring and new managers is an
introduction to management. Such a programme would be
particularly helpful if it included three additional compul-
sory modules. A women-only course would give women a
better understanding of the real issues of working in a man's
world and of how to avoid, or deal with, the unseen
obstacles and discrimination they might encounter. By providing strategies for them to cope with a male culture and
male managers, whilst at the same time showing them how
to put into practice a positive image of the corporate culture,
a more balanced management style should emerge. Understanding the different ways in which men and women use
words and body language, learning how to counter aggressive behaviour in a constructive manner, and having the
confidence to present their views and to demonstrate their

successes will lead, in time, to these behaviours becoming natural and habitual.

A second module – for men only – would concentrate on training men to recognize the capabilities and contributions of their female colleagues and, consequently, how to work more effectively with their female peers and their female subordinates.

The third module would then be able to consolidate and capitalize upon the previous learning to focus on how men and women could work together in a creative and productive way, realizing that they will all have both masculine and feminine traits within them. Acceptance of this and of the fact that it *is* possible to work in partnership together, by being true to themselves and their individual managerial styles, moves away from the establishment of a competitive relationship to one which acknowledges and values differences.

For one manager, 'my ideal world would be one which celebrates neither sex is better or worse than the other; and that "masculine" and "feminine" behaviour is more helpful as a distinction than "man" or "woman", "strong" or "weak" and so on'. There is a general feeling that both men and women have been victims of typecasting in the past and that it is now time to recognize that both sexes have the ability to adopt a wide range of masculine and feminine behaviours which all have their rightful place in a happy and successful working environment.

The significance of people who are responsible for recruitment within companies is evident. There is an increased awareness of the role that psychometric testing, for example, can play in assessing how groups work together. This is judged not only on the skills that individuals bring to a group, but also on their behaviours which determine how successfully the team achieves its purpose and goals.

Inevitably, the reasons for bringing men and women together in training sessions and the various methods of achieving this are expressed in many different ways. They vary from the suggestion of one of the interviewees that male managers should conduct courses which are attended by female managers only and where the men have to *listen*, as part of their brief, to the following statement, which puts the onus for change firmly on the women's shoulders: 'Men and women can and must learn from each other. If women are to get the "top jobs" of the future, then they will only do so if men give them up. That means men have to change to eradicate the present practice of "clone" appointment. Men will only change if women help them to change – they won't do it on their own because they have nothing to gain. Women have everything to gain and so must, once again, put in all the effort. We have to find ways of getting men to relinquish their power in ways that don't threaten their capabilities and in a way which will enable them to gain something'.

Understanding the different ways men and women use language is yet another skill which is coming to the fore. 'I have come to the conclusion that in order to be successful, women have to be "bilingual" – that is, they have to learn the male language *without* losing access to their own. Deborah Tannen, in *You Just Don't Understand*, describes the "two languages" particularly well.' Being aware of the variance in style and acquiring some of the skills to manipulate the 'other' language – for example, good public presentation skills – is as important as many other basic management skills.

Assertiveness and confidence-building are also mentioned as areas in which many women would benefit from additional training, but there is an increasing feeling that many men now are as much in need of these skills as the women. The balance between the training and development opportunities offered to men and women is beginning to even out to the point where, in some cases, 'I believe we risk a backlash from male colleagues, particularly those who feel blocked in their own career progression, in that they feel that the current concentration on women's training needs is not fair'.

Case study – Julia

Julia, 39, is married to an Army Officer and has two young children. She was educated at Benenden, has a degree in Experimental Psychology with Statistics from Oxford and an MBA from INSEAD. She is a partner in an international executive search firm, and for a long time was the only woman partner worldwide. She has recently moved to the division specialising in the recruitment of non-executive directors.

'Benenden was not just academic – it also instilled the expectation that women should have a career. I was not hugely academic and rather surprised everyone when I gained a place at Oxford. I didn't have any particular idea about what I wanted to do afterwards and I found Oxford to be only so helpful with careers advice and I left without a job. I called a few advertising agencies, but they advised me to get some work experience. So, for a while I sold advertising space for a publication, before becoming a sales manager for a new database for Prestel and suddenly I began to realize what I *didn't* want to do.

'I still wanted to go into advertising and joined one of the big agencies as a graduate trainee in 1980. My three years there gave me broad exposure to the various types of clients, and I became responsible for a wide range of people in my team. I enjoyed the work but, towards the end, there were frustrations. I was interested in the wider aspects of the clients' business and found the agency's perspective rather narrow. When I expressed an interest in strategy consulting, my father suggested I talk to the senior partner of McKinsey, who recommended going to business school first. I applied to INSEAD, lived with my parents in Brussels for six months to polish up my French, and in 1984 won a women's scholarship for the MBA – I hadn't even known there was a women's scholarship until they told me on the closing date.

'Having qualified, I wrote, on the strength of that course, to all the major strategy firms and Bain offered me a summer job. I was given a project of my own and, on the basis of its success, they offered me a full-time job. It was good experience and gave me credibility, but I'm glad I'm not doing it now. I knew I wasn't playing to my strengths. There was no thought given to the people side and that, together with the fact that my social life was on hold, made me think, "I'm not prepared to go on living like this".

'I looked into the HR field and a headhunter asked me if I'd ever thought of being in executive search. When I told Bain what I was thinking of doing, they suggested that I set up a HR strategy operation for them, but at the same time I realized they weren't wholeheartedly committed. I thought again about headhunting – wondering if its image would mean a downwards career step – but joined Egon Zehnder in 1987 and it's definitely proved to have been the right move for me. It plays to my strength of client management. I've become very good at coping with the whole range of business issues and at asking questions.'

Do women need to compromise to succeed in a male-dominated corporate world?

The answer to this question depends a great deal on how the traditional male culture is defined. It may be, for example, that such a culture is one of long hours and hard work and people who are not seen to work to the accepted pattern are criticized. This may be appropriate when managers within that culture are under pressure and are pulling their own weight, but it is not fair on colleagues if they behave otherwise. However, it is possible for women managers to assert their own perspectives and behaviours in a way in which they feel comfortable. Many women believe that traditional management practices of control no longer work, as such methods assume a static world and must therefore be modified or become extinct as different skills are required. If, as current trends suggest, confrontation and adversarial attitudes are becoming less useful, those men and women who are able to demonstrate more co-operative behaviours will be called upon to put these skills and attitudes into practice.

The business world seems to be moving away from the idea that women have to be 'honorary men', even though this was a characteristic of the generation which entered the work market around the 1950s. Women have also observed that in the 1980s many female managers did succeed where others had failed by adopting a male style, but have concluded that this was not to be helpful for women in the long run.

One manager who had observed the behaviour of some women who thought that they needed to act, look and sound like men commented, 'Most men react violently against such behaviour, and other women are not impressed either. It's difficult to find the balance and some-times you can even be insulted for assuming a normal female perspective. I've often found the pejorative 'mother-hood' statement levelled against my views – in fact, "motherhood" is thought of as a soft perspective. Do they know about mother tigers, I wonder?'

There is another belief that women who adopt a male style and culture too completely actually disable them-selves, because 'moving away from an "authentic" style induces high stress levels and has consequences on the ability to relate to and manage people. Women who do this are often resented by both men and women'.

There are still many women managers who feel it is necessary to adopt male characteristics to be successful –

not showing emotion, always having to show that they know the answer, not being able to admit to mistakes – but, at the same time, there is a definite move towards individuals making their own choices about how they behave at work. Clearly, it cannot be ignored that successful women have to compete in a male-dominated culture. 'The ability to progress and have influence is about accepting that it is a male culture, *but* also about adopting personal strategies which enable you to work within it. These include empathizing with the senior men whilst demonstrating that your female perspectives and skills will enable you to help solve their problems'. Yet, as one manager says, 'There is a sense that even men find it tough living inside a culture that does not recognize the human element of the importance of trust, relationships, etc to get things done. I believe women have an enormous opportunity to influence and bring their perspectives to bear if they *choose*. The question is whether sufficient women wish to take on the challenge of leadership rather than remain followers'.

The approach adopted by many women – but not accepted by all – is to fit in with the present culture until they have been accepted and then, once they have made it, begin to break the stereotypes and challenge the system's foundations and values. 'I think that often one has to work within a particular culture in order to gain credibility before asserting something different. However, I don't think this means taking on male characteristics.'

There is an optimistic note creeping into discussions about women's role in management. 'Gradually, senior managers are realizing that they need a balance at the top in order to retain that balance throughout the company. They need the hard-edged "males" who concentrate on results – plus the people-oriented "females" to ensure the successful management of people.' With the growing acceptance that male and female traits are found in both men and women, many organizations are demonstrating that the integration of a variety of styles does not involve relinquishing important differences.

The ideal outcome is for women to retain their femaleness, despite the difficulties. This also presents problems for the men and an interesting and salient point is made by one manager: 'We must recognize the torment this can pose to men. It's easy to accept a single, lesbian, childless woman as a freak. It's far harder to accept an overtly heterosexual, feminine woman – complete with partner and children – because this suggests to men that *their* wives and girlfriends could do the same. It makes them feel very vulnerable'.

The issues of 'balance' and 'valuing differences' again come to the fore in discussing whether women have to compromise in order to succeed in a male-dominated corporate world. Many women state that the choice of management style is not a case of 'either . . . or'. Instead, women firmly believe that what they have to offer is rooted in their difference and are keen that their acceptance goes hand in hand with their male colleagues' wish to work together as equals. 'It's our unique qualities that should make every organization positively desire to have women working at the highest levels.'

As women begin to make their own decisions about the way they wish to manage and as their confidence grows in using systems for their own ends, companies will give them scope to do more. 'The question will be whether the organizations choose to materially reward these new approaches. (Job evaluation certainly isn't coping any longer). If they don't, I believe that women will continue to do what they've started to do already, i.e., either go to a more sympathetic organization, or start one of their own.'

Women who have spent a considerable number of years working their way up through the ranks, and who have attained a senior position where they are able to contribute fully to the organization's success, have faced the challenges of operating in an alien environment. They have achieved this by learning how to develop a range of behaviours whilst remaining 'true to themselves', by knowing when to use the appropriate behaviour, and by encouraging and promoting the benefits of diversity. They measure their success in a variety of ways: 'I think I've been successful because women in roles such as "project co-ordination/strategy/support" are perceived to be less threatening than men in these roles and are able to move things along, be supportive, coax and cajole so that the tasks get achieved with men's egos still intact'.

If women have difficulty in finding a company culture which values them, a professional woman encourages them to be entrepreneurial in this situation: 'Find a position of influence, or power, so that you can turn the tables around. For many years I worked in a male-dominated profession. I've now moved away from the practice and enjoy being out of the fray, but I'm still engaged in the same issues having established a career as a private and public client'.

A seat on the board?

If the natural progression for a manager is to become a director and, ultimately, a board member, and acknowledging the fact that a very small percentage of boardroom places in the UK are occupied by women, what are the chances of women moving into the boardroom?

The overall impression is that things have still a long way to go. Broadly speaking, the two main reasons for the lack of female representation are that men, who dominate boards, don't recruit them and that women, for various reasons, are often not available.

A universal, reflex reaction to the question: 'Why aren't there more women board members?' is, 'Because men recruit in their own image'. The widely-held belief is that the old boys' network and the inclination to bring in 'clones' still prevails and, that until men are educated to understand that there is value in diversity in the direction-giving process, they will continue to replicate themselves at Board level. This is tied in with the traditional male-dominated culture of organizations and, as women's presence becomes more prevalent and their abilities and talents are viewed as a threat, some men will try to prevent women taking hold rather than seeing it as an opportunity to learn different ways of operating.

Where personal recommendation to the board is still the norm, it doesn't occur to many male directors that women would be of the right calibre and, even if it does, they often don't know where to find appropriate candidates. Much of this has an historical background. Most executive directors come from either general management or financial backgrounds – traditionally male preserves – and this is where the bulk of board members have spent their careers. Even with today's more open and professional recruitment of non-executive directors, the specifications remain conservative and tend to require executive director experience – a catch-22 situation.

Women, as already mentioned, have not in the past had the confidence to push themselves forward as forcefully as their male colleagues, and it is only in the last few years that women have begun to put their names down on registers which deal with non-executive directorships, members of public bodies and so on. There are a growing number of organizations who operate these types of registers, networks and associations, which encourage their members to use their skills and experience in this direction.

Another reason explaining the smaller supply, or low profile, of women when it comes to recruiting board members is their comparatively late arrival at the top of their businesses because they've taken career breaks, have started on a specific career path several years later than their male contemporaries, or have not had the same promotion opportunities as their male colleagues. The fact that many women have additional responsibilities to children and other domestic duties, leads some men to conclude that they would not be fully committed to board work. The loud riposte to this from successful women is: 'Untrue – we'd try even harder to make up for it.' I was appalled to learn of several examples of male executives discussing the unreliability of women in senior positions because of school holidays, sickness and so on. One woman reported overhearing a man say, 'Women in the workforce are useful for only three weeks of every month'. Where these attitudes prevail, education and proving ability by example is going to be a long and uphill struggle.

All this assumes, of course, that women want to move up to board level. From the women's point of view, taking on board responsibilities does not always look the golden prize that it is purported to be. Indeed, many of the reactions would probably surprise and shock the men. For example, 'As boards are dominated by a few (rather stuffy) men, it would probably be *really* tedious working with them' and, 'Much boardroom business can be seen as boring'. The boardroom is still perceived to be a predominantly macho domain which functions on male lines and women cannot easily flourish in this environment without great personal sacrifice. They do however realize that, if this is to change, the effort will have to emanate from them and it will probably come about when we achieve a generation of career-oriented women who reach board level without it being any more of a fight and/or remarkable than it is for the men.

It is true that the family factor is still key, and that women think carefully about maintaining a balance between their personal and professional lives. The sheer amount of time and energy the top board jobs require allows very little flexibility and those women with young families would invariably choose not to compromise the needs of their children.

There is plenty of discussion about how women are less prepared to devote themselves completely to work at the expense of personal lives. One manager observes: 'Women managers I admire have multi-faceted lives – which means that they are not focused solely on their work, although it has a central role in their lives. Men's lives, on the other hand, can more easily and traditionally be set up so that all aspects – family, recreation, social activities – reinforce a man's role in business'. Where an organization's culture demands long hours of the people at the top and there are the attendant stresses and strains to contend with, many women are not prepared to put up with that alongside their other responsibilities as home-maker.

Also bearing weight in this argument is the view that very few women begin their careers with the top in mind and, in any case, they are generally more concerned with achievement rather than power and do not strive so aggressively for promotion for the sake of it and what it entails.

It is for this reason, one manager suggests, that women are increasingly moving away from working in large organizations to becoming consultants or setting up their own small businesses. She believes that it would be 'worthwhile examining the small business/consultancy world to see how many successful women have foregone institutional life in favour of greater flexibility and personal control'.

Opportunity 2000 is convinced that many women are frustrated by a business world still dominated by men and that is why they are leaving to set up their own businesses. This is confirmed by the various small-business divisions in high-street banks who have reported a noticeable increase in the numbers of women starting up on their own.

Sadly, many men are still bound up in the traditional view that women should be in a supporting role – especially when they have had enormous backing from their wives. As one woman says, 'Being a single parent, I can understand why they might want someone supporting them in the background. It would make my life a whole lot easier'.

An interesting point comes from a manager who suggests that women aren't pushing down the doors to boardrooms because it is not clear what being a director means and what makes a successful director. And it is certainly true that we are in the midst of a huge rethink about the way organizations are run and the whole subject of corporate governance is under review. The Institute of Directors, amongst others, is devoting a great deal of time and energy to this subject with the aim that board members may become better able to understand and fulfil their roles as direction givers.

What are the chances of this situation changing significantly in the next decade?

There are some glimmers of change on the horizon, but the general feeling is that it could take as long as ten years for the way organizations are run to modify enough to make it attractive for women to want to play a part as members of the board. As most of the issues which currently prevent them becoming board members are predominantly women's issues, they recognize that most of the initiatives for transformation will have to be taken by them. 'Much, therefore, depends on how active this present generation of women who have made breakthroughs into senior and top management jobs are willing to be, and how effective they are as mentors, coaches and policy makers.'

The improvement may seem slow, but the women in their thirties and forties who are coming through into top positions, together with the new generation of men who are more used to the idea of working alongside women, are pointing the way forward. The cultural changes and re-modelling which will result from these new working practices and the increasing numbers of men who are 'on our side' will surely make a difference to the representation of women at the top of organizations? As women grow more confident in their abilities and become a stronger force in the workplace, a more 'equal opportunities' approach to people at work will develop and men's and women's careers will one day be considered equally important.

As more women seek a 'career to the top', their influence will affect the way that boardrooms function; as will greater flexibility in working conditions, which will enable women to take on more responsible positions. Issues of help with childcare and domestic duties are likely to become less pressing at a senior level, because in most cases the women have older children who have either left home or who do not need constant attention or they earn enough for the expense not to be a problem. However, for the majority of working mothers there will always be a need for appropriate childcare and other support services, so the demand for their improvement will continue.

Women are encouraging and supporting each other more to increase their visibility and business profile – 'More obvious and inspiring role models will help both men and women to understand the exact nature of the contribution and value of women in the boardroom'.

The non-executive route could be extremely useful to women who wish to be involved in the running of businesses, as many boards are now actively seeking female non-execs. One director sees this as a very positive step: 'Having had board experience in this way, or through setting up our own companies, we are more likely to have credibility when we apply for executive positions and chief executive posts'.

Another describes her own position and its potential drawback as she contemplates becoming a non-executive director: 'I can see a trend increasing whereby women (particularly those with young children), who do not think they could cope with a more senior job *and* a home/family, find themselves in senior advisory positions. Although we have considerable influence and power – working as we do for some very senior men – we lack line-management account-ability and, to some extent, credibility. It feels like a trap – reasonably well-paid, acceptable hours, interesting work. A good way of training to be a director but, if we wait too long, will anyone ever employ us as one?'

ACTION PLAN:

1 Think about the skills that you bring to the workplace – how do they contribute to the success of your organiz-ation and how do they complement those of your col-leagues, both male and female?
2 What do you need to equip yourself with for the demands of work in the 21st century? Build on your strengths, but don't ignore the areas you're less comfortable with – you may be pleasantly surprised to find that they are interesting and actually help you to understand other aspects of your work.
3 Be true to yourself – don't act differently at work in an attempt to emulate other managers if this is not your natural style.
4 Where male colleagues need help in developing different ways of managing as we approach the new century, be generous with your assistance.

And, finally . . .

As we approach the Millennium, attention concentrates on fresh beginnings, the dawning of a new era, and exciting opportunities and challenges. How can we ensure that such talk is transformed into action?

This is the ideal time for women managers to stake their claim to be part of the transition from outmoded and restric-tive management methods to an open and honest attitude which encourages a climate of learning, discovery and achievement. Corporate cultures need to minimize the gap between male and female managers by recognizing and valuing different management styles as complementary, not divisive. Women can be the driving force in facilitating the changes by using their full range of talents and qualities.

Not only are women ready and poised to take their rightful place in the world of work, but organizations cannot afford to lose women managers or stop attracting women managers in the future. Business success in an increasingly competitive world will depend upon an organization's ability to offer a fair and balanced future to employees with greater emphasis being given to the 'softer' management qualities many women possess – such as nurturing and coaching staff, sensitivity and perception when dealing with clients and colleagues, attention to harmony between work and home which results in mutual benefits. However, such success can only be achieved as and when companies allow women to create their careers on an equal platform with men. Women need to feel that they are reaping the rewards for all their hard work and they are asking for recognition of their achievements.

The climate for change is upon us and the younger generation of women managers are striding forward with new confidence and greater opportunities than ever seen before to break down the barriers that have previously hindered women's progress and fulfilment in management.

We must allow women to make their contribution to corporate life, while maintaining the balance between body, mind and spirit. By setting this example, women will also give permission to their male colleagues to follow the same path. Women are ready to make their contribution. Are organizations ready to meet the challenge?

APPENDIX I

THE CASE STUDIES

The interviews I conducted during the course of my research provided a rich variety of material. The case studies relate the different ways by which these women have arrived at their present positions, the people and events that influenced them, and how they each view the future. There are several common threads running through the stories which may be a source of comfort, or perhaps inspiration, to other women who might feel uncertain that they are following their appropriate career path.

One factor which emerges clearly from these case studies is the way in which women's careers often develop. It is said that, by the time they reach senior management level, women have often had a much wider experience than men in equivalent posts and I think this is well demonstrated in the studies.

I trust their accounts and comments will encourage existing managers – both male and female – to continue the progress that is under way and inspire new and potential managers to consolidate the rightful position of women in the workplace. I also hope that they will make those people who are responsible for the development of employees, whether line managers or providers of training and development, become more aware of what they can do to obtain the best out of a crucial element of their workforce and ultimately their organizations.

Here is the 'last word' from the case study interviewees who were happy to share their views of their futures:

Alison has recently relinquished some of her voluntary positions and chairmanship of City Women's Network. She feels the time has come to devote more time to herself and looks forward to taking on a non-executive directorship. Her goal is now to do an MBA.

Judy sees her current job as an ideal way of training to be a director, or chief executive. 'It has reinforced my belief that, in future, work will spread increasingly across sectors and will involve doing things through and with others. My experience in the private, public, academic, European and now health sectors has given me the confidence to know that I could manage a senior director or chief executive role in any such organization. However, I am keenly aware that the opportunities are few and that the male stereotypes of these roles are not the style I would wish to follow. My next step is therefore a very difficult one and I'm not even sure that a job exists yet which would enable me to do what I want. The challenge for me then is to create one and, in doing so, hopefully enable the energies of many other men and women who feel similarly frustrated by the current systems of working to be released in order to develop a much healthier world than we have now.'

Carol has a plan. 'I am saving money so that when the children are older they can go to university, because there may not be sufficient grants then. I'm also saving some for myself. At the moment, my children are the most important thing in my life and my time and money are tied up with them. As long as I am learning and meeting challenges, that's OK for the next eleven years. When my daughter is eighteen, I will only be forty-nine – which is not old. When the children first leave home, what I might do is go to France so they can visit me there. In eleven years' time, I'm going to travel and, since I made that decision, I'm so much happier as I now have a long-term goal. I'm learning the piano and when I've mastered that I'll learn the guitar. Music is a great way to meet people. I'm going to learn French and Spanish, because I want to go to Latin America as well. I will never stop learning.'

Returning to work fairly recently means that **Beverley** feels her confidence has dropped a little, but she is finding her feet again. 'I look round now – I'm well-paid, I like my colleagues and there are new challenges. We will wait and see what happens. Perhaps I will look into doing a course in psychology and counselling.'

Theresa has experienced two years of uncertainty as her Company has merged with another of a completely different culture. Sadly, not only is her future with that organization unclear, but it also appears that under the 'new' structure most of the senior women seem to have disappeared. 'I would like to do one of the two jobs I've been interviewed for. If not, I will become a consultant because I don't think I would want to be employed by anyone else. I had in mind that I wanted to do something else when I retire and I might just have to bring that forward a bit. I would like to concentrate more on writing, because you can do that for a long time. The children are doing well – so I don't have to worry about them.'

Another interviewee who has recently moved into a new job, which she sees as the next step on her road to the most senior level in her field is **Zoë**. She values the balanced partnership she has with her husband and will continue to be truer to herself at work.

Sarah's road map is always planned five to ten years ahead. She is now confident that, despite all the setbacks and hard work, she can build her business. 'By the year 2000 my business will be *something* in corporate PR for the high-tech industry. I want Bourneriver to stand for quality. Running your own business is a mirror – it says everything about you as a person. I probably need to go into a strategic alliance in a few years' time, which will allow me to take a year off – I want to sail round the world.'

Julia has recently made an internal move into the area of the recruitment of non-executive directors and chairmen. 'I see this move as a good step.'

APPENDIX II

THE SCOPE OF THE QUESTIONNAIRE

The sample chosen for the questionnaire is not large. It does represent, however, a wide range of jobs, ages and qualifications, and the combined experiences and influences cover a period of some forty years. The relevant details about the respondents to the questionnaire are as follows:

Total number of respondents: **33**
based in the UK: 28
based in Hong Kong: 3
based in the USA: 1
based in New Zealand: 1

Numbers in each age group:
21–30   1
31–40   8
41–50   19
over 50   5

Examples of job titles held by respondents:
Area manager
Chief executive
Consultant

Director
Partner
Personnel manager
Quality adviser
Service delivery manager

Numbers in each work sector:

education:	2
private sector:	13½
public sector:	14
(local government: 7)	
(health service: 7)	
self-employed	2½
voluntary/charity:	1

Range of qualifications:

Accountancy
Architecture
Art
Business Studies
Drama
Engineering
History
Law
Management Studies
MBA
Nursing
O and A levels
Physiotherapy
Psychology
Secretarial
Social work
Teaching

Positions held outside work:

Associate/consultant

Charity/voluntary
Non-executive director
School governor
Women's networks

APPENDIX III

Many of the quotes and examples I have used in this book came from completed questionnaires.

Although the questionnaire is detailed and takes some time to fill in, the women said they found it thought-provoking and useful.

I hope you have found the issues raised in this book interesting and have enjoyed reading what other women say and feel. If you would like to add your thoughts to my research, please complete the questionnaire and return it to me direct (3 Beresford Terrace, London N5 2DH). I would be most grateful to receive your comments.

QUESTIONNAIRE

QUESTIONNAIRE

1   Name

2   Position in Organization

3   Organization

or Self-employed ☐
(please tick if appropriate)

4   Contact Address

Phone: **Fax:**

5   Affixes (eg, BSc; FIPD; ACCA; FRSA; etc)

6   Do you hold any other positions?

(e.g., non-executive director)

7   Age Group   (please tick appropriate box)

21–30 ☐   31–40 ☐   41–50 ☐   over 50 ☐

8   Education/Training   (please indicate level attained)

Secondary   O level ☐   A level ☐

Tertiary ☐
(please list)

Professional ☐
(please list)

Other ☐
(please list)

9 Can you draw your career path?

or Please list the jobs you had before taking up your present position (starting from now and working backwards, with dates)

10   **Has anything stood in the way of your
     achieving your career goals?**

No ☐ If 'No', please move on to question 11

Yes ☐ If 'Yes', please elaborate

11   Have other people been particularly helpful during your working life?

(e.g., mentors or coaches, official or unofficial)

No ☐ If 'No', please move on to question **12**

Yes ☐ If 'Yes', please elaborate and indicate any women with an asterisk

12   Have you found any books/articles/other sources of ideas or information particularly useful during your working life?

No ☐   If 'No', please move on to question **13**

Yes ☐   If 'Yes', please list and say why

13 Have you attended any courses/programmes that were particularly helpful or inspiring?

No ☐ If 'No', please move on to question **14**

Yes ☐ If 'Yes', please list and give reasons

13a   Were any of the courses designed specifically for women?

No ☐   If 'No', please move on to question **14**

Yes ☐   If 'Yes', please say which ones

14 **What is your opinion on courses run for women managers only?**

15 **Could more be done in the area of training and development for women managers?**

No ☐ If 'No', please move on to question **16**

Yes ☐ If 'Yes', please give your views

16 **According to the Institute of Management's** *Management Development to the Millennium,* **managers in the next century will have to be good at:**

- **strategic planning**
- **responding to and managing change**
- **total quality management**
- **verbal communication**
- **coaching others**
- **delegating responsibility**

Have you any comments on this list of skills, with particular reference to women managers?

No ☐ If 'No', please move on to question **17**

Yes ☐ If 'Yes', please elaborate

17   There is much talk about the dilemmas and
      compromises facing women executives and
      managers in the male-dominated corporate
      world.

      Do you have any comments to make on
      the suggestion that women managers are
      more likely to progress in, or have an
      influence on, an organization if they accept
      and adopt the traditional male culture
      rather than assert their different female
      perspectives and behaviours?

No ☐   If 'No', please move on to question **18**

Yes ☐   If 'Yes', please elaborate

18   Would you describe yourself as a successful manager?

No ☐   If 'No', please say how you will recognize when you are successful

Yes ☐   If 'Yes', please say how you measure that success

19 **A small percentage of boardroom places in the UK are occupied by women (probably about 2%).**

Do you have any views on why this is so?

No ☐ If 'No', please move on to question **19a**

Yes ☐ If 'Yes', please elaborate

19a **Do you have any views on how this situation may change in the next 5–10 years?**

No ☐ If 'No', please move on to question **20**

Yes ☐ If 'Yes', please elaborate

20   I know these questions cover only the tip of the iceberg. Is there anything else you'd like to say before posting this back to me?

ADDITIONAL INFORMATION

It would be of help to have some extra personal information about you if you are prepared to let me have it. I will quite understand if you don't wish to complete this section.

1 **What are your current domestic arrangements?**

a living with a partner ☐

b living on own/sharing with others ☐

c single parent ☐

d how many children? ☐

e what are their ages? ☐

f do you have any extra help, for example with children or housework? ☐

If 'Yes', please specify:

2   Do you have any other comments or observations on how your life is organized which may be relevant to this survey?

I would like to discuss these issues further.

Yes ☐   No ☐

Please phone me on

CONFIDENTIALITY:

Please indicate below how confidential your answers are:

☐ You may use all the above details without asking further permission.

☐ Please clear with me before using my name/ organization.

☐ Do not identify me under any circumstances (but you may use the data).

Many thanks for your time and for giving me the benefit of your experience and opinions.

© Sally Garratt, 1998

FURTHER READING

Books: A small selection mentioned more than once by the women I have spoken to.

Lee Bryce, *The Influential Woman: How to Achieve Success in Your Career and Still Enjoy Your Personal Life* (Piatkus, 1994)

David Casey and David Pearce, *More than Management Development: Action Learning at General Electric Company* (Gower Press, 1977)

Clarissa Pinkola Estés, *Women Who Run with the Wolves: Contracting the Power of the Wild Woman* (Rider, 1993)

Charles Handy, *The Age of Unreason* (Arrow, 1995)

Charles Handy, *The Hungry Spirit: Beyond Capitalism – A Quest For Purpose in the Modern World* (Hutchinson, 1997)

Margaret Hennig and Anne Jardin, *The Managerial Woman* (Pan, 1979)

Rosabeth Moss Kanter, *Men and Women of the Corporation* (Basic Books, New York, 1993)

Max Landsberg, *The Tao of Coaching: Boost Your Effectiveness at Work by Inspiring and Developing Those Around You* (HarperCollinsBusiness, 1997)

Judi Marshall, *Women Managers: Travellers in a Male World* (John Wiley, 1984)

Judi Marshall, *Women Managers Moving On: Exploring Career and Life Choices* (Routledge, 1995)

Deborah Tannen, *You Just Don't Understand: Men and Women in Conversation* (Virago, 1992)

Jean Wollard, *Daughters and Mothers* (Thorsons, 1995)

Bulletins and Reports:

Bulletin on Women and Employment in the EC
Quarterly bulletin containing statistics and comment on women's employment in the EC. Available from Manchester School of Management, UMIST, PO Box 88, Sackville Street, Manchester M60 1QD

The Diversity Directory: A Guide to Equal Opportunity Trainers and Consultants, (8th edn., 1995)
Compiled and published by Diversity UK, 3 Abbey Square, Turvey, Bedford MK43 8DJ (Tel: 01234 881 380)

Family Friendly Working: New Hope or Old Hype (1992)
Pinpoints the pros and cons for flexible and family friendly working. Good definitions and summaries. Available from the Institute of Manpower Studies, £30.00.

Industrial Relations Review and Report
Twice monthly bulletin on industrial relations and other employment issues.

The Key to the Men's Club: Opening the Doors to Women in Management T. Coe, (1992)
A one-off report based on a study of Institute of Management members, both men and women. Good numerical data.
Available from the Institute of Management.
(Tel: 01536 214 222)

Institute of Management:
Management Development to the Millennium (1996)
> Available from the Institute of Management, 2 Savoy Court, Strand, London WC2R 0EZ (Tel: 0171 497 0580)

A Question of Balance? A Survey of Managers' Changing Professional and Personal Values (1997)
> The IM was supported by FI Group plc in writing this report.
> Available from the IM (as above), or FI Group plc, Campus 300, Maylands Avenue, Hemel Hempstead, Hertfordshire HP2 7TQ. (Tel: 01442 233339)

Mary Parker Follett – Prophet of Management: A Celebration of Writings from the 1920s, Pauline Graham (ed.), (Harvard School Business Press, 1995)

Men and Women in Organizations, Tom Boydell and Val Hammond (eds.),
(MEAD Special Issue, Summer 1985, Vol 16, Part 2)
> Interesting to look at issues raised over a decade ago.
> Available from AMED, 15 Belgrave Square, London SW1 8PS. (Tel: 0171 235 3505)

Recruiting and Retaining Women
A survey of practice from a report called *Recruitment and Development* published by Industrial Relations Services.

Social Focus on Women
Central Statistical Office (now the Office for National Statistics).
> Available through HMSO.

Women Singled Out: A Survey of Women's Views on Women-only Development Training, Jenny Daisley and Liz Willis (The Springboard Consultancy)

Available from Springboard, 2 Atcombe Terrace, South Woodchester, Stroud, Gloucestershire GL5 5EP. Tel: 01453 878540.

The Springboard Consultancy has recently published the results of a survey it carried out on this subject and gives an alternative perspective to the opinions I found when talking to women managers.

Additional information on Skill Swap may be obtained from Sally Fraser, or Rick Stein, at the Salomons Centre, Broomhill Road, Southborough, Tunbridge Wells, Kent TN3 0TG Tel: 01892 515152, Fax: 01892 539102).

More details on this type of programme, which also includes thorough de-briefing sessions, may be obtained from Suzie Morel, Corporate Health Consultants, The Old Rectory, St Brides Super Ely, Cardiff, South Wales CF5 6EY (Tel: 01446 760813, Fax: 01446 760050).

USEFUL ADDRESSES

Ashridge Management Research Group
Ashridge Management College,
Berkhamsted,
Hertfordshire HP4 1NS
01442 841177/843491

Association for Management Education and Development
15 Belgrave Square
London SW1X 8PS
0171 235 3505

British Chambers of Commerce
Manning House,
22 Carlisle Place
London SW1P 1JA
0171 565 2000

British Women Pilots' Association
Tren Grove,
Nanty Derry,
Gwent NP7 9DB
01873 880278

Business and Professional Women UK Limited
23 Ansdell Street,
London W8 5BN
0171 938 1729

Centre for Research on European Women
22 rue de Toulouse,
1040 Brussels,
Belgium

City Women's Network
PO Box 353,
Uxbridge,
Middlesex UB10 0UN
01895 272178

Equal Opportunities Commission
Overseas House,
Quay Street,
Manchester M2 3HN
0161 833 9244

Employers for Childcare
Cowley House,
Little College Street,
London SW1P 3XS
0171 976 7374

European Commission
Directorate-General for Employment, Industrial Relations
and Social Affairs,
Jean Monnet House,
8 Storey's Gate,
London SW1P 3AT
0171 973 1992

They also run *Equality Exchange* which is an employers' network for sharing good practice and keeping abreast of the latest legal and practical developments in equal opportunities. Membership is open to employers, trainers and consultants.

European Women's Development Network
c/o EFMD,
Rue Washington 40,
Brussels B-1050,
Belgium
00 32 2 648 9385 in Belgium
01227 265969 in UK

Family Policy Studies Centre
231 Baker Street,
London NW1 6XE
0171 486 8211

The Fawcett Society
5th Floor,
45 Beech Street,
London EC2Y 8AD
0171 628 4441

Gingerbread
16–17 Clerkenwell Close,
London EC1R 0AA
0171 336 8183

Industrial Society
3 Carlton House Terrace,
London SW1Y 5DG
0171 839 4300

They operate the *Pepperell Network* which is open to any working woman.

Institute of Directors
116 Pall Mall,
London SW1Y 5EA
0171 839 1233

Institute of Personnel and Development
IPD House,
Camp Road,
London SW19 4UX
0181 946 9100

Institute of Employment Studies
Mantell Building,
University of Sussex,
Falmer,
Brighton,
Sussex BN1 9RF
01273 686751

Local Government Management Board
Arndale House,
Arndale Centre,
Luton,
Bedfordshire LU1 2TS
01582 451166

Management Centre Europe
rue de l'Aqueduc 118,
B-1050 Brussels,
Belgium
00 32 2 543 21 00

New Ways to Work
309 Upper Street,
Islington,
London N1 3BH
0171 226 4026

Opportunity 2000
44 Baker Street,
London W1M 1DH
0171 224 1600

Royal Society for the Encouragement of Arts, Manufactures
and Commerce (Women's Advisory Forum)
8 John Adam Street,
London WC2N 6EZ
0171 930 5115 Extn. 237

Springboard Consultancy
2 Atcombe Terrace,
South Woodchester,
Stroud
Gloucester GL5 5EP
01453 878540

A well-established womens' development consultancy
which has been used by many Opportunity 2000 companies
and which is also operating internationally.

'Take Our Daughters to Work'
252b Grays Inn Road,
London WC1X 8JT
0171 402 5363 (Mon–Thurs only)

Development Unit on Women in SET
Office of Science and Technology,
Queen Anne's Chambers,
28 Broadway,
London SW1H 9JS
0171 210 0538

Women and Property
19 Store Street,
London WC1E 7DH
0171 255 3396

Women in Banking and Finance
55 Bournevale,
Bromley,
Kent BR2 7NW
0181 462 3276

Women in Construction
169 Quarry Street,
Liverpool L25 6DY
0151 428 1329

Women in Management
5th Floor,
45 Beech Street,
London EC2Y 8AD
0171 382 9978

Women Returners Network
8 John Adam Street,
London WC2N 6EZ
0171 839 8188

Women in Science and Engineering (WISE)
The Engineering Council,
10 Maltravers Street
London WC2R 3ER
0171 240 7891

Women's Engineering Society
Imperial College of Science, Technology and Medicine,
Department of Civil Engineering,
Imperial College Road,
South Kensington,
London SW7 2BU
0171 594 6025

INDEX

achievement 80, 121
Action Learning 68, 77
advertising 113
After School Clubs 22
Alison 22–5, 27, 42, 55, 88, 128
ambition 105, 121
analytical skills 99
appraisal 78, 83, 106
articles 56–7, 60, 142
Ashridge Management Index 106
assertiveness 22, 40, 109, 112
Association for Management Education and Development 54, 161
associations 54, 119, 161–2
attention to detail 102
attitudes 6, 17, 35
  men's 18–20, 109–10
  of organizations and managers 8, 18–25
  of young people 9–10

balance, see home/work balance
banking 49–50, 54, 62–3, 89–90
Barnes, Brenda 5
barriers 17–44, 105
barristers 20, 31–2, 49
Beverley 36, 45–7, 55, 87, 129
boardroom 20–1, 118–24, 150–1
books 56–8, 60, 142
BP 31–3
Brown, Gordon 22
Bryce, Lee 58
Business and Professional Women 54, 162
business start-ups 10, 103, 121

Cadbury Committee 21
Cap Gemini 90, 91–2
career 29–30
  barriers 17–44

career – *cont.*
  breaks 17, 36, 75, 91,
    119
  consultants 29
  goals 18, 25–35, 43–4,
    105
  managing 105
  path 15–17, 30, 60, 127,
    139
  planning 17, 105
  portfolio 28
careers advice 15, 17, 18,
    25–35, 38, 43, 103,
    105–6
Carol 19, 38–9, 42, 52,
    64–5, 128–9
Central Statistical Office 63,
    67
chairmen 3, 20
change 63–79
  in management style 1, 3,
    5, 10
  managing 95–7
  in organizations 1–2, 4,
    100
childcare 6, 22, 108, 123
children 39, 50, 60, 86–8,
    91, 98, 120
City Women's Network 54,
    162
Civil Service 42
coaching 17, 51–3, 122
  and confidence-building
    11
  as management skill
    95, 98, 99, 100,
    125

  by older female manager
    9, 21, 122
  specialist consultancies
    106–7
colleagues:
  relationships with 80–1
  support from 47–50, 54
committees 56
communication 95, 98, 99,
    100
compromise 114–18, 148
conferences 55, 69–70, 78
confidence, *see* self-
    confidence
consensual management 98,
    100
consultants 52–3, 54, 67,
    106, 121
counselling 105, 107
courage 99
courses 58–60, 64–6, 143
  men-only 111
  women-only 65–6, 71–9,
    110–11, 144–5
  see also development;
    training
Cranfield School of
    Management 70
credibility 124
culture, corporate 1, 74,
    124–5
  challenging 40
  changing 22, 96, 100
  and compromise 114–18,
    148
  feminine 3, 11, 71
  and inclusion 48

male 2, 11, 16, 18, 33, 40,
    80, 110, 114–16, 119
customers 81

delegation 95, 98, 99
dependants 36, 37, 108
design 61–2
development 110
    developmental
        management style
        101–2
    improving 104–14, 146
    personal development
        plan 106
    programmes 58, 60, 65,
        67–8, 143
difference, valuing 109,
    111, 117
directors 7, 20–1, 53, 106,
    118–24, 128
discontent 5–6
diversity 48
domestic violence 37
down-sizing 21, 53
dress 59

Eastern Gas 62
The Economist 33, 57
education 41, 102–3
    careers in 34–5
    innovative 64–5
    limited 30, 35, 36
    open learning 109
    see also school; university
elderly dependants 36, 37
Elward, Margaret 79
entrepreneurship 24, 118

equal opportunities 6, 42,
    104, 110, 123
equal pay 82
Equality Exchange 163
Estés, Clarissa Pinkola 58
European Women's
    Development Network
    54, 163
expectations 105

family:
    and career choice 26,
        35–6, 43–4
    expectations and
        pressures 35–9, 105
    obstructive 36–8
    supportive 50, 60
    see also home/work
        balance
family-friendly organization
    6, 10, 37
Family Health Support
    Agency 47
feedback 80–1, 83
femaleness 22, 72, 117
financial reward 81–2, 84
financial skills 99
flexibility 96, 109, 123
Forbes, Sheila 100, 101
Forgan, Liz 70
friends 54, 88
Fritchie, Dame Rennie 70

GEC 68
glass ceiling 17, 33
goals 18, 25–35, 43–4, 81,
    83, 140

graduates 7, 16, 18
Gray, John 57
guilt 107

Harvard Business Review 57
Hay, Susan 6, 22, 108
help, *see* support
Henderson, Elisabeth 76
home-making skills 95
home working 2
home/work balance 22, 43,
    60, 86–92, 125
  directors and 120–1
  and guilt 107
  men and 101
  multi-priority juggling
    36–7
  and personal support
    systems 107–9
  as skill 67, 96, 99–100
  and stress 6
  and success 81, 83
Horlick, Nicola 5
hotel industry 36, 45
Howe, Lady 7
Huff, Professor Anne 70
human resources 16, 18,
    114

image consultants 59
imagination 99
inclusion 48
income 81–2
industry groups 54, 107
influence 80, 99
The Influential Woman
    (Bryce) 58

Institute of Directors 122,
    164
Institute of Management 5,
    27, 37, 95, 99, 147
Institute of Personnel and
    Development 54
integrity 107
interpersonal skills 97–8
interpersonal support
    systems 109–13
isolation 21, 53, 56
IT 38–9, 41, 90, 106

Jackson, Glenda 70
job security 28–9
job swaps 109
joint working 100
Judy 20, 31–5, 48–9, 55,
    128
Julia 26–7, 50, 74, 113–14,
    130
junior management 15

knowledge 44, 60, 64, 78,
    100

language, male and female
    112
language skills 100
late development 17, 30,
    36, 119
law 20, 31–2, 48–9
learning 64–5, 79, 81
legislation 19
Leiden 77
leisure 6, 59, 60, 67,
    91

life skills 95–6
line manager 5, 51, 124, 127
literature 56–8, 60, 101, 142
local government 16, 19, 33–4, 46, 85–6, 104
Lyons 61–2

McKechnie, Sheila 70
male/female balance 10–11, 35, 116
management:
  attitudes 18–25
  barriers 17–44
  changing styles 1, 3, 5, 10, 101
  routes into 15–16, 18
Management Development to the Millennium 5, 95, 147
Management Today 70
marketing 54
MBA 32, 55, 62–3, 64, 70, 74, 114
media 38
meetings 102
Melanie 89–92
men:
  and change 112, 124
  and family 6, 101
  'honorary' 8, 21, 115–16
  male backlash 112
  prejudices of 18–19, 118–20
  working with 101, 109–13

Men are from Mars, Women are from Venus (Gray) 57
mentors 17, 53–4, 68, 91
  and confidence-building 11
  informal 60
  older female manager as 9, 21, 122
  specialist consultancies 106–7
middle management 5, 7, 17
multi-cultural management 100
multi-priority juggling 36–7, 97

networking 54–6, 60, 66, 68
  and confidence-building 11, 56
  support networks 105–7
  via professional bodies 69
  via women-only programmes 71
NHS 55, 104
  courses 58–9
  development programme 68–9
  managers 16, 19, 46–7
  nursing 23
  Women's Unit 69
nurseries, workplace 108

obstacles, *see* barriers
openness 71, 72

Opportunity 2000 7–8, 121,
    165
optimism 10, 116
opting out 16–17
organizations:
    attitudes of 18–25
    changing 1–2, 4, 6, 100,
        122
    see also culture, corporate
outdoor activities 69
outside activities 58–9, 60
over-compensating 87

parenting 6, 95, 98
part-time work 2, 22
partners 87
Pearson Group 3
people management 102,
    116, 125
PepsiCo 5
performance 101–2
personal development plans
    106
personal life see home/work
    balance
personal limitations 18,
    40–4
personal support systems
    107–9
personnel 16, 31–2
politics, internal 17, 40, 63
portfolio career 28
power 99, 112, 121
PR 103–4
professional bodies 54, 69
professional support systems
    105–7

promotion 19, 63, 67, 79,
    85, 119, 121
psychometric testing
    111
public sector 16, 110

A Question of Balance 8,
    27–8, 37
questionnaire 131–55

Rank Group 45
Recess College for Senior
    Executive and
    Professional Women
    76–8
recruitment 111
redundancy 29
refresher courses 75
registers 119
relationships 80–1, 83, 98,
    116
reputation 80, 83
respect 84
rewards 84
risk 78, 100
rites of passage 75
role models 9, 44, 51, 60,
    72, 73, 80, 123
ropes course 69
Royal Society of Arts 54,
    165
rules 41–2

Salomons Centre 68, 69
Sarah 27, 41, 49–50, 88,
    98, 102–4, 130
Scardino, Marjorie 3

school 3, 105
  career's advice 26–7
secondment 68, 100, 109
secretarial training 15, 23,
  103
self-awareness 77
self-confidence:
  confidence-building 11,
    44, 74, 56, 59, 72, 112
  fragility of 80
  lack of 17, 30, 40
self-criticism 82, 84
self-employment 2, 10
self-esteem 56, 101
self-organization 102
self-worth 84
seminars 69
senior management 9,
  47–8, 53
  courses 68, 73–4
  female 7, 44, 49, 66
  Recess College 76–8
sexual discrimination 19
Skill Swap 68–9
skills 17, 78, 124, 147
  hard and soft 83, 96, 125
  life skills 95–6
  for next century 95–102
  training 60, 64, 66–7
  underestimating 40, 44
Social Focus on Women 63,
  67
Social Trends 27 1–2
society 104
speech 59
staff relationships 80–1,
  98–9

status 79, 82, 84
stereotyping 95, 110, 111,
  116
strategic planning 95, 96–7
stress 6, 34, 85, 89, 100,
  115
success 79–86, 118, 149
support 44–63, 123, 141
  interpersonal systems
    109–13
  personal systems 107–9
  professional systems
    105–7
  skill of 98
  woman's supporting role
    121–2

Tannen, Deborah 57, 112
Theresa 26, 41, 42, 53,
  61–3, 64, 87, 129
time management 102
The Times 3
total quality management
  95
training 63–79, 92
  external 68
  improving 104–14, 146
  in-house 66, 67
  introductory 110
  reasons for 63
  re-training 29
  right, finding 65–70
  skills 17
trust 34, 69, 71, 116
TSB 62–3

university 26–8, 31

values 81
Vaz, Patricia 70
Vinnicombe, Dr Susan
　　70
voluntary sector 25

womanliness, *see* femaleness
women, help from 44–5
'Women in Management'
　　conference 70
women's issues 20

*Women Who Run with the
　　Wolves* (Estés) 58
workforce, women in 2,
　　7–8
workshops 69

Yorkshire Bank 8
You Just Don't Understand
　　(Tannen) 57, 112

Zoë 41, 50, 84–6, 129

The Tao of Coaching

Boost Your Effectiveness at Work by Inspiring
and Developing Those Around You

MAX LANDSBERG

Coaching is *the* key to unlocking the potential of your people, your organization and, ultimately, yourself.

The good news is that becoming a great coach requires nurturing just a few simple skills and habits.

Max Landsberg, responsible for professional development programmes at McKinsey & Co in the UK, takes you through the stages needed to master and implement coaching to maximum effect. He shows how to:

- nurture an environment where coaching can flourish

- develop a team of people who relish working with you

- enhance the effectiveness of others through learning

- create more time for yourself through efficient delegation

By investing small amounts of time to provide constructive feedback, mentoring and encouragement, managers can substantially boost both their colleagues and their own performance.

With the current emphasis on helping individual employees to realize and deliver their full potential, the techniques of coaching are fast becoming essential tools for managers and other professionals. This is the first book which, in a highly entertaining and practical way, shows how to go about it.

'I'm making this useful guide required reading for my executive team'
GEORGE FARR, VICE-CHAIRMAN, American Express Company

'Practical, readable and relevant'
ARCHIE NORMAN, CHAIRMAN, Asda Group plc

0 00 638811 6

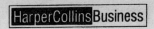

Jamming

The Art and Discipline of Business Creativity

JOHN KAO

No corporate asset is at once so prized and yet so poorly managed as the imagination and creativity of a company's people. In today's competitive environment, companies who understand how to manage creativity, how to organize for creative results and who willingly implement new ideas will triumph.

John Kao, who teaches creativity at the Harvard Business School, offers an approach that demystifies a topic traditionally confounding to business people everywhere. Drawing an analogy, Kao illustrates that creativity, like the musical discipline of jazz, has a vocabulary and a grammar. He explains how creativity needs a particular environment in which to blossom and grow. Like musicians in a jam session, a group of business people can take an idea, challenge one another's imagination, and produce an entirely new set of possibilities.

Jamming reveals how managers can stimulate creativity in their employees, free them of constraints and preconceptions, and guide them instead to a chosen goal where imagination is transformed into competitive supremacy. Using specific examples from a wide range of companies – including Coca-Cola, DreamWorks SKG and Sony – *Jamming* is a fascinating study of the shape and relevance of this most valued commodity in the workplace of the future.

'No matter how much you've downsized, or reengineered your company, all those efforts don't mean a thing if you ain't got that zing . . . *Jamming* serves as a primer on how to nurture talented workers . . . Kao's message is sound'

Fortune

0 00 638682 2

HarperCollinsBusiness

The Fish Rots from the Head

The Crisis in Our Boardrooms:
Developing the Crucial Skills of the Competent Director

BOB GARRATT

An organization's success or failure depends on the performance of its board – an ancient Chinese saying is that 'the fish rots from the head'. Yet the vast majority of directors admit that they have had no training for their role and are not sure what it entails.

As boards' activities are made more and more transparent under national and international law, there is an urgent need for a transformation in the way directors' competencies are developed.

Bob Garratt argues that directors need to learn new thinking skills to apply to the intellectual activities of direction-giving and implementing strategy. They need to develop a broader mindset to deal with the uncertainty of higher-level issues such as policy formulation, strategic thinking, supervision of management and accountability.

The Fish Rots from the Head is the first book to clarify and integrate the roles and tasks of the director and provide a programme of learning. As the tide of regulation swells, no board director can afford to ignore it.

'An important contribution to the corporate governance debate and clear and intelligent advice on how to improve the performance of a board'
TIM MELVILLE-ROSS, INSITUTE OF DIRECTORS, London

'This clear, very readable book should ensure that many more fish swim rather than rot'   SIR MICHAEL BETT, CHAIRMAN, Cellnet plc

0 00 638670 9